Financial Advice
for
Blue Collar America

KATHRYN B. HAUER, CFP®, EA

ISBN: 0-9912413-1-2
ISBN-13: 978-0-9912413-1-6

COVER DESIGN BY

*Art*Mishel

TABLE OF CONTENTS

CHAPTER 4. COLLEGE AND TECH TRAINING
BENEFITS OF A BLUE COLLAR CAREER

DISADVANTAGES OF BLUE COLLAR WORK

PAYING FOR COLLEGE & TECH TRAINING

PREFACE

I grew up in a blue collar family, fighting for space in a row-house by a steel mill with a dad who hadn't finished 8th grade and a mom who was a nurse before nurses had college degrees. Blue collar in the past could mean a difficult life for you and limited opportunities for your family. Today, however, blue collar careers can offer high salaries and interesting work. I've got sound financial advice for blue collar individuals and families; I also see new opportunities emerging for blue collar wealth. That's why I wrote this book. In my case, I moved out of the working-class sphere into the white collar world through educational opportunities, but I see great value in continuing or starting a blue collar career. This book covers financial basics, discusses the fundamentals of investing, looks at ways to avoid financial scams, considers the value of college and how to pay for it, explores trends in blue collar employment, and offers practical tips on how to make the most of your financial life no matter where you work.

INTRODUCTION

The basics of financial health cut across all walks of life and all levels of wealth. Sound financial behavior involves spending less than you earn, saving money for the future, managing the risks of life with the right amount of insurance, legally minimizing taxes, and investing the money you save wisely. Why this book then, with a focus on blue collar workers? And what does blue collar mean?

In categorizing people, you risk stereotyping and thus minimizing their unique and valuable characteristics. However, distinct groups share common problems, and it's helpful to find answers to that particular set of questions in one place. Blue collar workers sometimes find themselves in the enviable position of having great income but lacking access to pertinent financial information that answers their specific questions. You can find that information here.

For the purposes of this book, "blue collar" means people who do more physical work than desk work at jobs that don't require a four-year college degree. I'm talking about skilled, trained workers who perform jobs that require the use of their bodies and their physical energy in addition to their brains. That job set includes trades people (carpenters, ironworkers, cement masons, pipefitters, operators, laborers, etc.); transportation workers (truck drivers, public transportation workers); automotive technicians; radiological and other technicians; workers in the oil and gas industry; healthcare technicians; police and safety workers; enlisted military personnel; and others. I also include manufacturing (factory) work to some extent, although some portion of factory work falls into an unskilled category that this book doesn't address. Many of the blue

1

collar jobs presented here require extensive training and apprenticeships, but none require a bachelor's degree. In this book, I focus on these types of jobs; other categories such as retail workers, food service workers, etc. perform valuable services and can certainly benefit from the concepts covered in this book, but their needs and concerns are not specifically addressed here. Also, at one time, nurses didn't need to have college degrees and made up most of the female portion of the blue collar workforce, but today's nurses must have college degrees. Other health care workers who require training but no college degree fall into this definition of blue collar.

Americans began using the phrase "white collar" as early as 1910; the term "blue collar" came into existence around 1924. Both phrases gained traction after World War II. For those who have only a passing knowledge of what "blue collar" means, a general sense that blue collar jobs are dying or dead sometimes prevails. That sentiment couldn't be further from the truth. Although the U.S. has become a "service economy" where we focus more on doing things for people than on making things, our need for people who physically work to build, create, maintain, and repair tangible objects is actually thriving. The U.S. Bureau of Labor Statistics expects that by 2020, 25% of new jobs will be in construction, healthcare, and trades.[1] The jobs are out there now, and more will be available in the future. It makes sense: no matter how many phone apps we use or how much entertainment we view, we will continue to need buildings to sit in, vehicles to move us, roads to drive on, and appliances to work for us. All of those useful items eventually break or wear out, and many systems and services need human decision-making to complement robotic technology.

What kind of jobs are out there in the blue collar work world? In 2016 and for the future, there are lots of interesting, high-paying, enduring blue collar careers. These jobs cut across many different types of industries and economic sectors. The first eight blue collar jobs on the following list have the most workers nationwide (2014 data)[2]; the remaining jobs show pay rates for other great blue collar jobs:

1. Maintenance mechanic ($40,687 or $19.56 per hour)[3]
2. Aircraft mechanic ($56,850 or $28.29 per hour)
3. Transportation maintenance ($65,770 or $31.62 per hour)
4. Heavy mobile mechanic ($51,778 or $20.38 per hour)
5. Motor vehicle operator ($45,000 or $21.64 per hour)
6. Electronics mechanic ($52,420 or $25.21 per hour)
7. Electrician ($52,910 or $25.44 per hour)
8. Gas plant operator ($63,398.40 or $30.48 per hour)
9. Electrical power-line installer and repairer ($64,990 or $31.24 per hour)
10. Nuclear power reactor operator ($82,270 or $39.55 per hour)[4]
11. Elevator installer and repairer ($76,490 or $36.77 per hour)[5]
12. Police officer ($52,576 or $25.27 per hour)

Those rates are real eye-openers since many of us won't ever make that much money in a year even if we have college degrees and often even if we have a master's degree or PhD. Recent statistics reveal the depressing reality that as many as 40% of college graduates work at a job that doesn't require a college degree while also experiencing a drop in incomes from their peers of the last decade.

Another unfortunate – and inaccurate – meaning that has attached itself somewhat to the term blue collar is the concept of those workers as "lower class" or "uneducated." The media sometimes portrays blue collar workers as gullible country bumpkins. These characteristics couldn't be further from the truth. As I show in Chapter 6 of this book, blue collar workers possess intelligence and skills on a par with college-educated workers. Additionally, blue collar workers understand what it means to work hard and to make meaningful contributions.

Jeff Torlina, author of *Working Class: Challenging Myths about Blue Collar Labor* and advocate for blue collar workers, writes that "blue collar work in working-class culture…cannot be understood in simplistic terms. Not only is work multidimensional, with its meaning understood according to a number of factors, but it is also both negative and positive – often at the very same time and in a variety of ways."[6] He goes on to stress the vital connection that blue collar workers have to their jobs that can be missing in white collar occupations: "to the blue-collar workers interviewed, it was simply obvious that they perform work that is necessary, important, and worthy of respect. They see the entire process of production and recognize that every aspect of the production process is essential for it to work."[7] In any job, one individual may find greater purpose and meaning than others in the same field, but the blue collar worker often gets a more tangible opportunity to feel like an important part of the team.

Although there are many advantages to a blue collar career as I discuss in this book, in no way do I mean to discourage my readers or their children who want to go to college. A four-year college education can open doors for exciting careers and good salaries. However, it's simply not the only path to success.

Life is good in the blue collar world. Let's talk about ways to make it even better.

CHAPTER 1
FINANCIAL BASICS

Money can be a tough topic to talk about. A 2014 poll from Wells Fargo[8] showed that Americans would rather talk about sex, taxes, religion, politics, and death rather than money. That makes sense – people will tell you they are afraid to die, that they are pro-gun, or that they have a great sex life much more readily than telling you how much debt they carry or how much they've saved for retirement. Money is tied to such high levels of emotion – success, happiness, good parenting, love, control – that it's a loaded subject.

However, as history shows, when you keep quiet about a subject, it means that misconceptions about it grow. Before Masters and Johnson, we passed along unhelpful myths about sexual behavior. Before Ralph Nader, consumers had little recourse when a product turned out to be a lemon. Racism, religious intolerance, discrimination, and other taboo subjects were harder to talk about then than they are today, and lots of misinformation resulted. That's what happens when you don't talk about things openly.

And we're STILL not talking about money in the U.S. At a glance, it seems as if we are because of all the books, articles, TV programs, radio shows, and advertisements. Now that we have the internet, a verbal taboo is different than in pre-electronic days. We can access financial information easily, and the information there is usually accurate and true. But if we're new to the subject and its terms, the information we find can be misinterpreted. Since we aren't likely to talk about what we read and learn, we can make mistakes. We're afraid to discuss money with other people, so no one sets us straight. Or, like teenagers figuring out how romance works, we ask another un-informed person who doesn't really know the answer, and we mess things up even more.

Financial errors can hurt much worse than others. Most mistakes irritate and inconvenience us: it hurts to be rejected at a job interview, to choose the slow line in the grocery store, or to forget about garbage day. Financial mistakes, however, hit us right in the pocketbook and can sometimes be of a crippling magnitude. If you get hit with a $30 charge because you forgot you have to carry a $250 balance at your bank and you dropped below for one day, then ouch! - you won't ever get that $30 back. If you take money out of your IRA or 401(k) to spend but neglect to pay taxes on it, you can owe the IRS big penalties.

Experts in finance – just like those in chemistry or political science – spend a lifetime learning their subject. You don't have to be an expert, however, to keep your money safe and help it grow. These basic concepts will provide a foundation for managing your money now and a springboard for learning more.

Accepted standards of financial planning look at these basic areas to determine financial health:

1. *Daily Finances* – net worth, cash flow, banking, budgeting
2. *Future Finances* – home purchase, college/training, and other goals
3. *Insurance and Benefits* – protecting yourself from loss; health, auto, homeowners, renters, union, Social Security, and other types of insurance and benefits
4. *Taxes* – tax preparation and refunds
5. *Wills and Estates* – what happens to your money and possessions when you die
6. *Investments* – building wealth (covered in Chapter 2)
7. *Far-into-the-Future Finances* – retirement planning and concerns (covered in Chapter 5)

The list above looks long and overwhelming, but if you think of financial health in terms of how you earn your money and how you protect it, all the steps above fall into place. These seven topics can be incredibly complicated or manageably simple. Let's talk about what each topic means and how you can get your arms around each task in your own life.

DAILY FINANCES

- Net worth
- Cash flow
- Banks and credit unions
- Earning interest
- Reducing debt
- Credit and debit cards
- Budgeting
- Emergency fund

Net Worth

Your net worth is defined as the monetary value of what you own. It's your assets (what you have) minus your liabilities (what you owe). It's helpful to calculate your net worth so that you can track how you are doing. Links to forms and spreadsheets are available in Appendix 1 of this book for formal calculations. You can also just do an estimate if you don't feel like dragging out all your financial information at the moment. To estimate, write down your assets: savings, investments, IRAs, 401(k)s plus the value of the major things you own (home, car, boat, land, furnishings). Then list your debts or liabilities: credit card balances, personal loans, student loans, auto loans, home loans, etc. Approximations are fine. Subtract the debts from the assets, and you've got your net worth. It may be negative, which is sobering but will show you the direction you want to head. Just as weight loss experts will tell you that it's simple to get in shape if you eat less and move more, financial experts can be just as callous: spend less and save more. If the simple advice those experts give were as easy as it is simple, we'd all be thin and rich. But it's not. We support ourselves and our loved ones in many ways – emotionally, spiritually, academically, and physically. When we are called on for financial support, it's hard to say no. That struggle can mean a low or negative net worth. The strategies discussed here will introduce you to the basics as you move toward positive net worth in your future.

Cash Flow

Net worth deals in the realm of the long-term. Cash flow is different from net worth in that it deals with immediate needs. Examining cash flow involves determining how much money is coming in and how much is going out. If more needs to go out than you've got coming in, you've got a problem. Again the simple "Spend less!" advice rings hollow when the kids are going back to school, the Kia needs a new transmission, your mother just broke her hip, and all three deer rifles were stolen out of the garage. You can shop at Walmart, request used parts, move your mother in with you, and (maybe) accept the fact that the freezer won't be stocked with venison this year, but even all that cutting won't completely eliminate the need for more cash to go out than is coming in. An essential part of financial health is figuring out what you need to change in your life to nail down this concept. All of us go through periods where we need more cash than we can generate. If you can spend less than you make most of the time, your savings will grow and you'll be able to invest for your future.

A circumstance somewhat unique to blue collar workers is the potential for intermittent cash flow. Some blue collar jobs are weather dependent: if it rains or snows, no one works and no one gets paid that day. Many blue collar jobs are project-specific, so when you come to an end of a job you may be out of work for a period of time. If you decide to return to civilian life after your enlistment period comes to an end, it may take you a few months to find a job. It will help your financial life if you can put away money to cover the periods when you are between jobs. I talk more about the emergency fund below, but it's important to have some money in savings to cover periods you are out of work.

Banks and Credit Unions

When you do save, a bank or credit union is the best place to put your savings. However, not everyone uses banks to the fullest degree possible. Take a look at these stats:

- About 22 million (8%) Americans don't have a bank or credit union[9]
- About 38 million (12%) are "under-banked" – they have a bank account but supplement their finances by using

expensive services such as a check cashing service, money order, pawn shop loan, auto title loan, paycheck advance, payday loan, and rent-to-own stores; rely on cash that is riskier because of possible theft and inability to prove payment; and fail to build the credit history they need for reasonable future loans.[10]

You need to open an account at a bank or credit union and use it for managing your finances. A bank or credit union can help you because it's safe, convenient, secure, and lower in cost than non-bank financial services. A good track record with banking helps build your financial future in a way cash can't.

Banks and credit unions are almost free or very reasonable in fees, but they are not without costs, especially when you break their rules. You can get hit with charges like these:

- Monthly service fee
- Minimum balance fee
- Automated Teller Machine (ATM) user fee
- Overdraft fee
- Stop payment fee
- Note: credit unions and online banks often have lower fees

You might be reluctant to use or count on a bank because of all these costs. I sympathize – the fees and rules are tricky, and I've lost money by not paying attention to changing rules at a particular bank. For example, my initial account at one bank I use for a business account required no minimum balance. Eventually that rule changed. I'm sure the bank sent me a letter telling me about the change, and I ignored it. As a result, I was out $45 for letting the balance drop below the minimum for one day in that month. I try to keep on top of all financial matters, but sometimes I miss things. In this case, that's what happened, and I paid for my mistake.

One way to avoid the minimum balance mistake is by using a credit union. If you qualify for a credit union in your town – because you work at a certain job, live in a particular zip code, or meet another qualification – you can make life easier for yourself because most credit unions have lower fees than banks. They also often require no minimum balance. You'll still be charged if you overdraft your account – only your mother might let you off penalty free if you exceed an actual balance! – but even in overdraft charges a credit union is usually kinder than a bank.

It's a good idea to set up a savings account and a checking account at the bank or credit union. You use the checking account for your daily and monthly bills, and you rely on the savings account as a place to save for emergencies and future goals. If you can have your paycheck automatically deposited in the bank or credit union with most of it going to checking but a portion going to savings, you can "trick" yourself into building an emergency fund. Once you've got three to six months of cash saved for emergencies, you can look into investing to grow your money.

What if your credit has become so damaged that you can't find a bank that will let you open an account? Banks check your financial history through a system called ChexSystems. If you have poor or damaged credit, the bank can legally refuse to let you open an account. It seems extremely unfair to me, but it happens. They can run a bank history report or an actual credit report (which doesn't count as a "hit" against your credit score). If you have had trouble with checking and savings accounts in the past, a bank could refuse you as a client. If you want to view your ChexSystems report or dispute your record, you can do that at the ChexSystems website (https://www.chexsystems.com). If you owe a bank money or have a bad banking history, it will be reflected there.

If you can't open a bank account, here are some ways you might be able to fix the problem:

- Go into the bank branch and talk with a banker there. The personal approach may work. Offer to bring in a paystub or a reference to convince the bank you are a good risk.
- Try other banks in town besides the one that just turned you down, talking to a banker at each one.
- Try on online bank like Etrade, Ally, or Synchrony.

- Try a credit union. Credit unions can be more lenient and more likely to offer second chances. You may have access to and eligibility in a local credit union or a national one like Navy Federal Credit Union if you were in the military.
- Work to build your credit history back up. That will take a little time, but you can do it.

Try not to berate yourself – it's a complicated financial world, and we ALL make mistakes. With patience and diligence, you can fix the problem, get a checking account, and improve your credit.

Earning Interest

Compound interest is a beautiful thing. Interest is the amount of money banks pay you for keeping money on deposit with them (or that you pay the bank when you borrow money). It's expressed as a percentage and can be compounded daily, monthly, or annually. When you deposit money in a bank that pays interest, you earn interest on the money you've deposited plus interest on the interest you earned earlier. It's a way that your money works for you when it's just sitting there. For example, if you take $100 (your "principal") and stick it under the mattress where it earns no interest, in 10 years you would have the same $100. If you were able to earn 5% interest compounded annually on that money, you'd end up with $162.89 at the end of 10 years, which is $62.89 more. If you'd started with $5,000, the resulting amount is $8,144.47 or $3,144.47 more. That's a big difference in results! As discussed later, finding a place that would actually pay you 5% in interest in 2016 without the risk of losing your principal is unlikely. Savers don't earn 30 years of risk-free, guaranteed 5% interest, but you get the picture of how compound interest helps you.

Let's change our compounded interest rate to a more modest and realistic 1% compound interest rate over 10 years. If you saved $100 you'd end up with $110.46 if your money were compounded annually ($10.46 more). The $5,000 example results in $5,523.11 or $532.11 more. Even though the returns aren't that great when you are earning 1% interest as compared to 5%, they result in your having money now that you wouldn't have if it sat in a jar. The additional amount earned at 1% isn't nearly as satisfying as the higher rate of 5%, which is why investors today may turn to riskier

11

financial vehicles like the stock market or corporate bonds for higher returns. Check out Chapter 2 for more information on these concepts.

In 2016, interest rates are low, which means you are not going to end up with nearly as much today as you would have in the 1970s for example, when interest rates – for both savers and borrowers – were much higher. Safe places to put your money – certificates of deposit (CDs), U.S. Treasury bonds and bills, money market accounts – pay such low interest rates today that they are not particularly successful vehicles for younger investors trying to grow their retirement funds. What's especially frustrating, as I discuss in Chapter 3, is that when you borrow money you *pay* interest rather than *earn* it: between 3% to 21% in interest on your mortgage loans, personal loans, and credit cards, and even higher interest rates on payday and title loans.

Reducing Debt

Not all debt is bad, and debt is probably necessary to achieve the goals you've established for yourself and your family. What and how much debt is ok? How can you reduce debt when you need to? Truthfully, it's not any easier than reducing your waistline. Both take discipline and sacrifice. Neither reduction experience is very fun. I find it hard to believe when people say that their diet or their frugality kick was "fun." To me, the *act* of learning how to do something well or taking yourself to new heights of suffering or sacrifice is not fun, but the *results* are incredibly enjoyable. It probably won't be fun to say no when your group is getting tickets to the game and you don't go because you want to save money. Eating peanut butter sandwiches you make at the house isn't as fun as eating Zaxby's wings. Wearing last year's dated winter coat when this year's styles are so awesome isn't fun. However, seeing your debt go down and then disappear is fun. Realizing rewarding results that you worked hard for is a great feeling. If you want to find ways to reduce debt, search the internet, go to the public or local college library, or grab a bench in the financial corner of Barnes and Noble – scores of people offer great advice on the topic. Appendix 3 also includes a list of helpful websites. Just be prepared for things to be tough as you work toward the very worthwhile goal of reducing and eventually eliminating debt.

Credit and Debit Cards

Credit and debit cards are useful tools for managing your money. A debit card lets you deposit and withdraw money and make purchases at retail locations. Debit cards only allow you to spend as much as you have in your account. A credit card lets you borrow conveniently, have money ready when you need it, especially in emergencies, and access a revolving line of credit. Credit cards require a minimum payment each month, but if you only make the minimum payment you incur a high rate of interest (between 13% and 23% or even more). Credit cards are useful because they help during emergencies; are safer and more convenient than carrying cash; allow you to make large purchases; help you build a financial credit history that in turn helps you get mortgages, home rentals, and insurance at lower rates; yield travel and other rewards; and let you spend money you don't have.

The primary disadvantage of a credit card is the same as its main advantage: it lets you spend money you don't have. That feature is crucial when your 27-year-old calls you from Bellevue Hospital in NYC after a midnight bike crash. Credit helps you buy an airline ticket on your home computer in South Carolina that puts you in NYC that same night. Credit allows you to spend a week there patching her up post-bike accident while you continue to spend even more money (on credit) you don't have. Credit buys the exorbitantly expensive return ticket too. During that worrisome week, credit is your friend. But next month when she's back to pedaling over the Williamsburg Bridge, credit cuts you like the middle school in-crowd. The credit card company wants you to pay them back. If you don't pay – or can't pay – you could end up paying far more than the actual cost of that bike accident. Months or years of just making the monthly minimum payment add a lot to that original bill when the credit card company is charging you 21% interest. I talked about how 1% or 5% interest can work for you in growing your money; it works even better for the credit card company's profits when they charge you 18% or 23%. Of those households carrying debt, the average U.S. household credit card debt stands at $15,863. Counting all households, average debt carried is $7,400. About 34% of Americans just make the monthly payment on their cards,[11] carrying debt from month to month.

Although you are certainly not alone if you are an American carrying credit card debt, it doesn't make your burden any lighter just because you are carrying it alongside of others.

The Problem with Credit Card Debt

When you borrow money for any reason, you pay interest to the lender as the fee for using that money. Interest rates vary depending on the prevailing interest rates in our economy and the type of debt you incur. Right now in 2016, we are in a very low interest rate environment, which means that is it relatively cheap to borrow money and, conversely, not as profitable to lend money. Home mortgage interest, for example, is very low today. When I was little in the 1970s, home mortgage rates were as high as 17%. Now they range between 3% and 4%. That means that, on a relative basis, less of your monthly mortgage payment is going toward paying your debt (the interest portion of your payment) and more is going toward the equity in your home. It's a great situation because you can buy more house at a 3% interest rate than you could afford at a 9% interest rate.

As a borrower, the lower the interest rate, the better, because you get to pay less for the privilege of using another's money. As a lender, the opposite is true: the higher the interest rate, the better. Lenders are legally permitted to charge higher interest rates, especially when they are at risk of not being paid back. When a lender loans you money to buy a house, the lender can always take back the house if you don't pay. When a lender allows you to buy things with a credit card, there is no "collateral" – no physical item – that the lender can take back if you don't pay. Since the lender has higher risk, a higher interest rate can be charged. In the case of credit card debt, you pay a much, much higher rate of interest than you do for homes, cars, student loans, home equity loans, or private bank loans. Credit card interest rates range from 12% to 23% and in some situations can be even higher. So when you only pay your monthly minimum on your credit card balance, you end up paying the credit card company a lot of extra money in interest. Here's an example: say the transmission goes out on the Rav4. It costs $1,500 to fix, which you don't have, so you put it on your MasterCard. Your minimum monthly payment is $50, and you pay that amount each month. If you didn't owe interest and you kept making the minimum payment, you'd have paid off the transmission in 30 months. However, as soon as you pass that first month, Capital One starts charging you 22% interest on your $1,500 charge. So if you didn't pay the bill in full for a year, you would have paid more than $1,800 for that transmission or over $300 in interest. Multiply that cost by many purchases over many years, and you see why credit card debt can cripple you financially.

Budgeting

Should you have a budget? Yes! Do you? Probably not. Only about 30% of Americans do. A budget helps you manage your cash flow. You can use fancy spreadsheets, internet programs, or paper and pencil to create and follow a budget, but all budgets basically employ four steps: record daily spending; record income; subtract spending from income; figure out ways to reduce spending or increase income. Part of the problem is that there may not be enough money to cover basic bills of living – income may be erratic; your job may pay inconsistently or be dependent on weather or management whims; or you may be out of work at the moment. Those situations make budgeting even more depressing than when you've got enough money. A valid budget requires you to record what you spend and how you spend it. Its collateral function is to slap you upside the head with the fact that you spend too much, often on frivolous things like Starbucks or shoes, in my case. When you create a budget and follow it, you take control of your financial future in a powerful way. See Appendix 1 for links to budgets and spreadsheets.

An Emergency Fund

You may have heard the term "emergency fund." In financial planning, an emergency fund is money set aside to cover items you haven't budgeted for. You build the fund in a savings account so that when a financial surprise crops up, you have money to cover it. Many folks live paycheck to paycheck, using all their income each month to cover their bills. When surprises occur, whether they are happy (baby, wedding, travel) or sad (job loss, breakage, illness, arrests), you've got money to cover them. If you are able, it is best to put aside some amount of money each month for emergencies until you have about three to six months of funds equal to your basic expenses. If your job is project-dependent, you'll want to have a larger emergency fund to cover the periods when you are in between jobs or if an extended weather delay prevents you from working and getting paid. Keep emergency fund money in a bank or credit union, and be sure to replenish as soon as you are able if you use it.

FUTURE FINANCES

I will give your far-into-the-future finances a whole chapter – Chapter 5 "Retirement" of this book. I talk about the decision about whether college is the right choice for you and your children in Chapter 4. Chapter 2 provides more advanced information on how to grow your money through investing. This section briefly covers the difference between saving and investing and what it means to save for a future financial goal.

Saving and Investing
Saving and investing are not interchangeable terms. When you save money, you know how much you will get when you take the money out. You don't expect that money to work for you and grow as you do with an investment. You save the money in a jar, in a checking account that pays no interest, or in a bank that pays very minimal interest. When you need it to pay for something, it's right there.

When you invest money, you put your money to work for you, hoping to get more money out in the future. You put your money in investment vehicles of varying levels of risk. You also commit to longer-term investments that have the potential to make money for you but may not be as "liquid" (or easy to quickly sell) as your savings. Even though you can turn your investments into savings later on (or vice versa), you invest with the direct purpose of increasing your money, so you are willing to let it be tied up for a period of time.

What are the best ways to *save* money? As discussed above, it's safer to keep your money in a bank or credit union than stashed in your house. It also helps to have a checking account that you use for paying bills and one or more savings accounts where you save money for future purchases. Savings accounts earn a small amount of interest, which is better than no interest. If you use coupons and look for deals when you shop, even small amounts of money matter to you and are worth getting. A savings account keeps your money "liquid" or easy to get to when you need it. This liquidity is the main difference between your savings and your investments. When you invest in certificates of deposits, bonds, real estate, or stocks (discussed in Chapter 2), you might not be able to sell those items at the moment you need the cash or if you do sell them, you could lose money or have to pay penalties. Your savings are accessible any time to pay for the things you are saving for: a vacation, wedding, repair, or other expense.

What are the best ways to *invest* money? You want to take your tolerance for risk into account when you choose investments, and you want to be sure to invest using reputable, trustworthy places. I talk about investing in Chapter 2 and keeping your investments safe from theft and fraud in Chapter 3.

INSURANCE AND BENEFITS

In addition to earning, saving, and investing money, you want to protect your money and your possessions. Insurance – for health, life, auto, possessions, home, business, bank accounts, ability to continue to work, getting hurt on the job, old age, unemployment – protects you in fair and necessary ways. Some types of insurance you pay for directly on your own; other types, such as workers compensation and welfare, are available to you if you qualify. I can't pretend that any of these insurances are "free," (a glance at your paystubs will remind you that you pay in plenty for the Social Security benefits you may eventually get!), but some types of insurance require you to make a choice to own them whereas others are chosen for you.

In this section, I'll discuss the following types of insurance and benefits:

- Health insurance
- Auto insurance
- Life insurance
- Homeowners and renters insurance

- Liability or umbrella insurance
- Business insurance
- Disability and worker's compensation insurance
- Unemployment insurance
- Bank account insurance
- Long-term care insurance
- Social Security insurance
- Other benefits that function as insurance: pensions, union benefits, military benefits, welfare, and food stamps

HEALTH INSURANCE

The following information on **health insurance** comes from the United States government healthcare marketplace, where you can find health insurance if you don't have coverage through a job, Medicare, Medicaid, the Children's Health Insurance Program (CHIP), your spouse or parents' plan, the military, or other source.[12] You can apply online, by phone, or with a paper application. When you apply, they will let you know if you qualify for:

- A health insurance plan with savings based on your income: most people who apply qualify for premium tax credits that lower the cost of coverage. Some also qualify for savings on deductibles, copayments, and other costs. All plans cover essential health benefits, pre-existing conditions, and preventive care.
- Medicaid and CHIP provide free or low-cost coverage individuals and families with limited income, disabilities, and some other circumstances. Some states are expanding Medicaid to cover all households below certain income levels – check your state to see if it is one of them.

You apply for insurance through the marketplace during certain times of the year, called open enrollment periods, unless you have a "qualifying circumstance" like a pregnancy, birth, death, divorce, or job loss. You can apply for Medicaid and CHIP any time of year. There's no limited enrollment period for these income-based programs. If you qualify, coverage can start immediately.

Most people must have qualifying health coverage or pay a penalty. If you don't have coverage in 2016, you'll pay a penalty of either 2.5% of your income up to the average yearly premium price of a Bronze plan or $695 per adult ($347.50 per child) up to $2,085 – whichever is higher. As of the writing of this book in 2016, you can call for more information about health insurance 24 hours a day, 7 days a week at 1-800-318-2596.

AUTO INSURANCE

If you've got a vehicle, it's likely that you already know a lot about auto insurance. Here's some additional information from the U.S. government website, *USA.gov*. Two factors determine what you pay for auto insurance: underwriting and rating. Insurance companies "underwrite" (a fancy term that basically means "figure out how much to charge for") the risk associated with an applicant, group the applicant with other similar risks, and decide if the company will accept the application. The rating and resulting cost is based on the claim frequency of the group or groups you fit into. If you are part of a group that statistically makes high claims, your insurance will cost more. Which groups might you be part of?

- *Your driving record* – drivers with previous violations or accidents are considered to be higher risk
- *Your geographic area* – urban areas have more claims than rural areas
- *Your gender and age* – males have more accidents; certain age groups have more claims
- *Your marital status* – married people show lower rates of claims
- *Prior insurance coverage* – if you have been cancelled for non-payment of premiums
- *Vehicle use* – higher annual mileage results in higher exposure to risk
- *Make and model of your vehicle* – luxury and sports cars average a higher number of claims[13]

If you fall into one or more of these categories, you'll pay more than a person who doesn't. You can minimize costs by changing some personal qualities, such as getting married, moving, or driving less. However, if you're a single man driving a new BMW who lives in Chicago and has already had a couple of accidents, your rates will be higher than a married woman with a clean driving record in a rural Nebraska town driving an old Kia. To minimize rates, shop around and ask for discounts, such as those for multiple vehicles, driver education courses, good student, safety devices, anti-theft devices, low mileage, good driver/renewal, auto/home package, and dividends. You need "collision" coverage, but you can save money on an older car by dropping the kind of coverage called comprehensive coverage, which pays for damage to your auto from causes like fire, severe weather, vandalism, floods, and theft. This coverage will also cover broken glass and windshield damage. Comprehensive coverage is less expensive than collision and is also optional. It's time-consuming to call or search on the internet for comparative rates, but you'll find you can save money by doing so.

LIFE INSURANCE
If you want your loved ones to have money when you die or if you want to provide a death benefit for them and possible cash benefits for yourself in retirement, you may want to buy **life insurance**. There are two main types: term and permanent.[14] Annuities have components of life insurance and investments, so they are covered in Chapter 2.

Temporary or "Term" Life Insurance
A term life insurance policy pays if the insured dies during the "term" of the policy. Term insurance is perfect for a young family who would suffer in the unlikely death of one parent because they depend on that income for basic expenses. Term life is affordable protection worth the cost of the premiums when you need to provide money for your family to live on if you die early. As a financial planner, I recommend term life insurance to most families with children and some couples. Term life doesn't cost much, but it protects your loved ones if an untimely death occurs.

Permanent Life Insurance
Permanent life insurance, the type of policy that offers investment features, combines the death benefit coverage of a term policy with an investment component that can build cash value over time. Unlike term insurance, all permanent policies remain in place as

long as the premium is paid. They also all have a cash value component that increases over time and allows the owner to borrow against that cash value.

There are four types of permanent life insurance:

- *Whole Life Insurance* – Offers a fixed premium for the duration of the policy, guaranteed annual cash value growth, and a guaranteed death benefit.
- *Universal Life Insurance* – Allows the policyholder to determine the amount and timing of premium payments (within certain limits) and to adjust coverage levels as needs change.
- *Variable Life Insurance* – Allows allocation of investment funds across stocks, bonds, or money market accounts with different levels of risk and growth potential; the use of equities raises risk for this type of insurance.
- *Variable Universal Life Insurance* – Combination of variable and universal life insurance that offers more flexibility in choosing investments; the use of equities raises risk for this type of insurance. Annuities are a kind of variable universal life insurance, and they are discussed in Chapter 2 in the investments section.[15]

How Much Does Life Insurance Cost?

A number of factors may affect life insurance premiums:

- The age you purchase your policy. The older you are, the more expensive the premiums.
- Your overall health. Life insurance companies typically ask you about your medical history, request access to medical records, and even obtain blood and urine samples for testing.
- Pre-existing and/or chronic health problems, such as diabetes, heart disease, cancer, or other diseases may prevent you from getting life insurance or place you in a high-risk pool at greater cost.
- Poor health habits, such as smoking and excessive drinking. Be aware that insurance companies may look back and consider these behaviors for the past five years.

- Engaging in dangerous hobbies such as skydiving, skiing, or rock climbing.
- Your driving record, in terms of accidents, DWI/DUI citations, claims, and tickets. The better your driving record, the better rates you'll receive for your life insurance.
- Your geographic area. Life insurance companies have access to regional data that document mortality rates and life expectancy, and they use that data to calculate the rates they offer.

Staying Safe When Buying Life Insurance

As a financial planner and consumer, I recommend and purchase term (or "temporary") life insurance as opposed to the different types of "permanent" life insurance discussed above. I personally feel as if the fees and charges associated with permanent life insurance (whole, variable, or universal) or annuities outweigh the earnings and potential benefits you are likely to get. However, many other financial experts think these kinds of insurance products are great. If you think permanent life might be right for you, do your research and make sure you choose a reputable insurance agent. Check the insurance company's credit rating. Through resources such as Standard & Poor's, A.M. Best Co., or Moody's Investors Services, you can see whether the annuity company you are considering has a solid credit rating. An "A+++" or "AAA" rating is a sign of strong financial stability. For more information, check the National Association of Insurance Commissioners (NAIC) Consumer Information Source (CIS).[16] The NAIC provides a database for consumers to research an insurance company's financial information and complaint data. The information in the CIS is supplied voluntarily by state insurance departments. Not all states provide the data, nor do all companies appear in the directory; however, it's a good place to start.

HOMEOWNERS AND RENTERS INSURANCE

An important type of insurance if you own a home is **homeowners insurance**. You're required to keep it during the life of your mortgage, and you want to make sure to continue to pay for it even when you own your home outright. Homeowners insurance is an important purchase because it protects one of your most valuable assets – your property – while safeguarding your personal legal responsibility (or liability) for injuries to others while they're on your property. Additionally, most mortgage lenders require you to have insurance as long as you have a mortgage and to list them as the mortgagee on the policy. If you let your insurance lapse, your mortgage lender will likely have your home insured. The premium may be much higher (and the coverage much less) than a policy you would buy on your own. The lender can require you to pay this higher premium until you get your own homeowners insurance again.

A homeowners policy usually covers:

- Your house and other buildings on your property
- Your personal property in your home or on your property
- Your personal liability (how much you have to pay for problems that occur)
- Medical payments for others accidentally hurt on your property
- Additional living expenses if you must rent a place to live while your home is being repaired[17]

If your home is insured on a replacement cost basis, then claims are paid based on the cost to replace your loss, not its market value. The replacement cost for a home is usually greater than the market value. If your policy is based on replacement cost, you must replace your property to be reimbursed; there are limits on the amount you can be reimbursed for your home.

A typical homeowners policy doesn't typically cover:

- Flood
- Earthquake, landslide, or mudslide
- Sewer backup
- Identity theft
- Dog bites
- Swimming pools or trampolines
- Operating a business from your home

If you've got a particular worry, you can buy coverage to manage that risk called a "rider." For example, you can buy flood insurance backed by the National Flood Insurance Program.

Apartment dwellers and other renters can buy **renters insurance** to protect possessions while renting. Many apartment complexes require this insurance; luckily, it's pretty cheap.

LIABILITY AND UMBRELLA INSURANCE

If you have substantial assets and high net worth, you may want to consider **liability or umbrella insurance.** Being insured for liability protects you from the risk that you could be sued and held legally liable for something such as injury, negligence, or malpractice. Liability insurance policies cover both legal costs and any legal payouts for which the insured would be responsible if found legally liable. For example, as a nurse employed by a licensed, insured facility, you technically don't need your own liability insurance more than what you currently have with your homeowners, but if you were an individual with a high net worth, you would want to be sure to protect those assets from someone suing you. It's unlikely that you would get in that situation, but you could have a car accident, have a worker injured while making a repair at your home, or have a visitor to your home injured that resulted in a lawsuit against you. The liability coverages you already have in place protect you. If you have many assets, you may want to consider an umbrella insurance policy to give yourself extra protection above the amounts in a standard insurance policy. The umbrella policy provides extra protection in the event that a lawsuit exceeds the basic level of coverage in the standard policy. An umbrella personal liability policy extends the basic coverage provided in different types of liability coverage, including home, auto, boat and tenant policies. This type of policy provides broad coverage, meaning that some claims that would not be covered by a standard policy may be covered under the umbrella policy. An umbrella policy only kicks in once the regular coverage amount is exceeded. Generally, the insured's standard policies must contain minimum levels of liability coverage that are specified by the insurance company in order to add an umbrella policy and the greater liability coverage that goes with it.

BUSINESS INSURANCE

If you have a business on the side, you'll want to buy business insurance to cover risks your business might face. Even if your business is small and home-based, you will still want to consider it. Cost and amount of coverage vary among insurers. The following types of business insurance are designed to protect your company from risk and you from having to pay out of pocket for a mistake or problem caused by your business.

- *General Liability Insurance* covers legal hassles due to accidents, injuries, and claims of negligence including bodily injury, property damage, medical expenses, libel, slander, the cost of defending lawsuits, and settlement bonds or judgments required during an appeal procedure.
- *Product Liability Insurance* protects from financial loss as a result of a defective product that causes injury or bodily harm.
- *Professional Liability Insurance* or *Errors and Omissions Insurance* protects against malpractice, errors, and negligence in providing services to your customers.
- *Commercial Property Insurance* covers everything related to the loss and damage of company property due to a wide variety of events such as fire, smoke, wind and hail storms, civil disobedience, and vandalism.[18]

WORKER'S COMPENSATION AND DISABILITY INSURANCE

Another key form of insurance protects you if you get hurt and can't work. If you get hurt on the job, you are automatically protected by **worker's compensation insurance,** which is paid for by the company you work for and is kept in place by our government. Federal workers are covered by a program administered by the U.S. Department of Labor.[19] Most other workers are covered by worker's compensation agencies run by the state where they live. In South Carolina where I live, the SC Worker's Compensation Commission runs the worker's comp program. The program in SC, as in other states, is in place to protect workers, encourage safety on the job, reduce dependence on charities, unify legal procedures related to on-the-job injuries, and prevent future accidents.[20]

Worker's comp only covers you when you can't work because you have been hurt while at work. However, if you get hurt when you are not at work or if you get sick and can't work, you can protect yourself from loss through **disability insurance.** The consequences of disability include the risk of loss of income and additional expenses for the care of the disabled individual. There are three primary options available to mitigate this risk:

1. Employer-provided Sick-Pay Plan and Group Short-Term and Long-Term Disability if offered. This option is best, but not everyone works for a company that offers this benefit.
2. Converting assets into sufficient income-producing assets. This option essentially means that you have reached a point where you could retire if you no longer worked or were unable to work for several months or years. You may be able to do this if you have assets that you can convert to cash to live on. After age 62 (or a few years later if you delay to earn a higher payment), you'll also have Social Security retirement payments coming in each month.
3. Personal Disability Income Insurance can be purchased to replace or supplement the group coverage within underwriting limitations of the insurance company. Social Security can also provide long-term disability payments, but these benefits can be difficult to qualify for.

UNEMPLOYMENT INSURANCE
Another automatic protection at work if you lose your job is **unemployment insurance**. Like worker's comp, as an employee you don't directly pay for this benefit. The U.S. Department of Labor in conjunction with the states administers this program, which provides unemployment benefits to eligible workers who become unemployed through no fault of their own and meet certain other eligibility requirements.[21] You need to apply for the benefits through your state unemployment office, and you usually need to show evidence that you are searching for a new job in order to continue to collect benefits. Unemployment benefits are generally not available to employees who are fired for cause. If you feel you were fired unfairly, contact the unemployment office and provide documentation to support your claim so that you can claim

unemployment benefits while you look for a new job. These payments are just a fraction of your regular paycheck, but the money will help while you look for another job.

Some blue collar workers, especially those in construction, will experience periods of layoff. As soon as you get your layoff slip, go online or go in person to your state unemployment office to start the process for getting benefits. You don't need to be unemployed for a long period of time to collect, and you are able to start and stop benefits if you pick up short-term work one week but then have no work the next.

BANK ACCOUNT INSURANCE

If you keep money in a bank or credit union, you want to be aware of the limits of Federal Depository Insurance Corporation (FDIC) or **bank account insurance**. This benefit insures up to $250,000 per owner against fraud, default, or bankruptcy by the bank. Note that stocks and money market accounts are not insured by FDIC; they are insured by the Securities Investor Protection Corporation (SIPC) up to $500,000 with specific requirements. SIPC insurance protects your investments from fraud or bankruptcy of the investment house that holds the investments, not the actual company you've invested in; it doesn't insure against losses you were to incur because of errors in your investment choices. For example, you were to use Etrade to buy shares of Nike stock and Etrade were to go bankrupt, SIPC insurance would help; if Nike were to go bankrupt, you'd lose all the money you'd invested.

LONG TERM CARE INSURANCE

A type of insurance that's becoming more popular is **long term care insurance** (LTCi). This insurance pays for nursing home or in-home custodial care if you become unable to care for yourself as you age. Medicare pays for medical care when you are 65 or over, but it doesn't pay for you to have paid help for your daily activities of life or to live in a nursing home. Appendix 3 lists safe websites to learn more about LTCi and links to companies who sell LTCi.

You want to choose a big insurance company that has been around for a long time and has a high A.M. Best rating[22]. A good rating gives you the best chance that the company will still be around, in business, and able to make good on its promise to you to pay for your long term care.

Not everyone needs LTCi. People with lower net worth and few assets and even some middle class consumers could find it difficult to pay the high premiums this insurance requires. Additionally, LTCi premiums can go up substantially in between renewal periods. Be sure to do your research before you buy. Appendix 3 provides good reference sites for comparing LTCi companies, costs, and benefits.

SOCIAL SECURITY INSURANCE

The payments and benefits you get from **Social Security insurance** can form an important part of your financial protection system as you age. Unless you are a Federal worker or worked for another special group, as a wage-earning employee, you have likely paid into Social Security your entire working life.

The Social Security Administration (SSA) is online, and workers can set up online accounts to access useful information. With an online account, you can see your projected benefits, check your earnings history, and research claiming strategies. Set up a *mySSA* account at www.ssa.gov. It's fast and easy. You enter personal information about yourself including answers to questions that only you are likely to know. Then you create a username and password. Keep in mind that if you've set credit freezes,[23] you'll need to remove them to create this account. The three credit bureaus (Experian, TransUnion, and Equifax) require separate freeze actions, so you'll need to remove and replace each of the three. You may have to pay a credit freeze fee as a resident of some states unless your state, college, Security Clearance authority, or primary shopping place (i.e. Target or Home Depot most recently) has allowed you to be able to waive the fee because your personally identifiable information (PII) has been hacked. If you are like me and live in South Carolina, attended the University of South Carolina, worked at the U.S. Department of Energy's Savannah River Site, and shopped at Target and Home Depot, that's five "we've been hacked" waivers right there! But you only need one.

Check Your Benefits and Earnings

Use your *mySSA* account to:

- Keep track of your earnings and verify them every year
- Get an estimate of your future benefits
- Get a proof-of-benefits letter if you are receiving them
- Manage your benefits:
    - Change your address
    - Start or change your direct deposit
    - Get a replacement Medicare card
    - Get a replacement SSA-1099 or SSA-1042S

Your online account will let you check to see if you have 35 years of earnings. Why is this number important? Your Social Security retirement benefits are calculated using a 35-year history of your earnings. It's important to note that it is not your *last* 35 years but your *highest-earning* 35 years. If you paid Social Security taxes for less than 35 years of earnings, the SSA plugs in zeroes for the missing years and calculates a 35-year average. You want to check your statements and do the best you can to make sure all your years of work are correctly listed. Few of us have records for how much we earned 30-some years ago, but you may notice a glaring error such as years missing for a period when you know you were employed. You may want to work a little longer to have 35 covered years and avoid any "zero-earnings" years.

Once you are online, you can see estimates of your future monthly retirement income based on three different ages when you might start your benefits: age 62, your full retirement age (age 66 for current retirees), and age 70. You can see how your monthly Social Security check increases if you delay the start of your benefits. If you are in the financial position to do so, you may decide to wait when you see how your benefits can increase.

An online SSA account can save you time and give you immediate answers to questions. However, an online account won't prevent every trip to the SSA office. You still need to go to an SSA office in person to apply for the Supplemental Security Income (SSI) program, which pays benefits to the disabled and those who have limited income and resources. You'll also need to go if you notice a mistake in your earnings or have a name change.

OTHER BENEFITS THAT FUNCTION AS INSURANCE

Other benefits you might be entitled to – pensions, union benefits, military benefits, welfare, heating bill assistance, food stamps, etc. – technically don't qualify as "insurance" but function as such to my way of thinking because they protect you financially and minimize risk. Some of these benefits are administered by the state you live in, so your first stop in doing research may with be with the state agency that handles human health and welfare and other social services or the local council on aging if you are in that demographic. You can also check with the reference librarian at the public library or college library. It's hard to ask for help, but safety nets are set up around you to catch you when you fall. In the 80 years of life that the average American gets, fortunes rise and fall. There is no shame in asking for help when your circumstances have turned for the worse.

TAXES

Income tax returns and all the information that goes along with doing taxes can seem overwhelming. You have to collect a lot of information in one place for yourself and your family members, and the whole time you're worried that there might be an unhappy financial surprise at the end. Will you owe money? Have you forgotten about income or dividends you earned? Did you tell your employer to withhold enough money to pay your taxes? It's always possible to make a mistake! For example, the year our daughter moved to New York City, she didn't check the box to withhold special city resident tax, and she ended up having to pay $1,700 in tax that she hadn't planned on that year. Sometimes an unexpected great year of income can cause higher taxes, especially if you worked as a consultant or did odd jobs on the side. An additional tax called the Alternative Minimum Tax (AMT) now affects middle-income taxpayers, taking away itemized deductions and raising tax bills in unexpected ways.

In addition to paying the taxes you owe, you may want to pay someone to do your taxes for you. Approximate tax preparation costs at national tax service firms (like H&R Block) range between $150 and $200 per return, depending on your circumstances. If you're running late, you'll pay those guys about $100 to expedite your return or about $50 to file an extension. It definitely pays to make sure you understand the preparer's fee schedule. Avoid preparers who charge based on a percentage of your tax refund. Using a paid preparer can help you maximize the deductions and credits you are entitled to, but the cost can be high depending on who you use. Below I talk about the possibility of preparing your own taxes as a way to save money.

Your options for getting your taxes done are:

- Use a free Federal tax return online service if you qualify (free state prep and filing is harder to find)
- Go to a Volunteer Income Tax Assistance (VITA) or Tax Counseling for the Elderly (TCE) site for free tax help (see Appendix 3)
- Do them yourself on paper
- Do them yourself using tax prep software (plan to spend about $60 each year for the software)
- Pay an online service to help or do your taxes for you and file them
- Pay an in-person tax preparer to do them for you

You want to make sure that you use trusted, reputable websites to do your taxes or learn about tax rules. I have to climb back on my "safe website" soapbox: be sure you are at a safe website before you believe what you read or enter personal information. You can count on websites with the extension (.gov), such as www.irs.gov. It's easy to type in the wrong address. The website IRS.**com** (as opposed to IRS.**gov**) isn't affiliated with the government at all, despite the misleading "IRS Tax Center" title in the browser bar and tab. The banner headline on the homepage also suggests an official association: "US Tax Center – Tax Information You Can Trust." The IRS says that "the official Web site for the Internal Revenue Service is IRS.gov, and ALL the IRS.gov Web page addresses begin with http://www.irs.gov." Most websites today are so well designed that it's easy to find yourself in the wrong places on the internet.

If you meet certain conditions or income limits, you might be able to have your taxes done for free and filed for free (see Appendix 3 under taxes). Now that we are in the electronic age, most people file an electronic return instead of a paper return, and that filing costs a fee for both state and Federal returns. In filing fees alone, if you need to do a Federal and a state return for yourself and your two children, that could be over $60 just in electronic filing fees, plus the cost of having the tax return prepared. If the amount you make (your adjusted gross income) is below certain amounts, you can access free tax software like FreeTaxUSA or the free versions of tax-prep software such as TurboTax, H&R Block, and TaxAct. These programs usually include free electronic Federal return filing. Additionally, depending on your age and income (for 2016 taxes, the income limit is generally $54,000), you may be able to use VITA, TCE or AARP free tax preparation, which is usually offered at the library or community center in your town.

What about doing your taxes yourself? With the many free and low-cost software options available to guide you through the process, doing your own taxes is a great idea for many people. Of course, many taxpayers are nervous about doing their taxes wrong and avoid doing them completely. But there's no reason to be afraid. It's not the end of the world if you make a mistake, as long as it's a mistake made in good faith, rather than intentional fraud. The IRS simply lets you know what you did wrong and how much you owe or will receive. A small, honest mistake doesn't generate an audit. If you've never done your own taxes before, now is a great time to learn. It will help you understand what you pay in taxes and why. Even if start them on your own and then end up paying someone else to do them, the exercise of learning how to do your taxes will make you a better consumer when it comes to negotiating costs when working with a tax professional. If you're able to do them on your own, you'll save money and gain real financial confidence.

If you decide to do your own taxes and need to buy tax prep software, you have several products to choose from, so make sure you do the research to determine which one is best for you. Most paid versions of tax-prep software are full of great information and education that will guide you step by step through the process.

When you use tax-prep software, you'll be asked questions that will help you pay the right amount of taxes and ensure that you don't make a mistake. You can also search online for information about the kinds of deductions and benefits you are eligible for in your particular situation. Be sure to keep all the documentation and forms you could possibly need when doing your own taxes. If you don't have a printer at home, save the electronic PDFs of your tax forms and worksheets to a thumb drive so you can take it somewhere to print all the forms. Also make sure to keep the CD or link to the tax-prep software you used. I always buy my tax software on a CD, which I save, rather than downloading it, in case I have to look back at a prior year's taxes and need a particular year of the software application. Why? If your computer crashes and you get a new computer, you could lose the downloaded tax preparation application for that tax year and your tax files. Keep all of your printed records and your thumb drive somewhere safe and accessible because you could need them when you do taxes for future years, if you want to apply for a loan, or for other reasons.

If you can become comfortable doing your own taxes, it can save you money in fees and make you feel more in control of your money. But if you need help, you can always turn to a qualified professional.

Should You Get a Tax Refund?

Many financial experts advise taxpayers to avoid getting a big tax refund. They make the valid point that it's silly to let the government use your money over the year for free. They say you should have access to that money all year, not just when you get your tax refund in the spring. They advise consumers to have less money withheld from their paychecks for taxes which in turn means more money each month to save and use. They say tax refunds aren't gifts: they mean you overpaid the government all year and that you are loaning the government money, interest free. Instead, many experts say, you should pay just enough taxes throughout the year to avoid a refund because you could have used that money to save, invest, or pay off debt. But in reality, for many Americans, the tax refund is an essential part of their financial lives and there are many reasons to continue getting a refund.

And all those financial experts are absolutely right, technically (just like all the other experts in parenting, health, dieting, and the countless other areas in which we are supposed to be doing right but can't always manage). If you're the kind of person who can keep a whole bag of Reese's peanut butter cups in the snack drawer without finishing them all in one sitting in front of *Game of Thrones*, their advice may be perfect for you. If you are that kind of a disciplined person with lots of self-control, that's great.

But what if you're like rest of us and don't have quite so much willpower? Temptation and risk have a lot to do with the pros and cons of getting a tax refund. Most Americans don't create and follow a budget – we are just winging it. If you don't have a plan for how you are going to use the extra money in your paycheck (as a result of adjusting withholdings to avoid getting a yearly tax refund), you'll probably blow it on shopping, going out to dinner, or the many other things that we blithely spend our money on. The theory that you shouldn't "let the government hold your money" seems less valid in our low-interest-rate world of 2016. For most of us, if we have an extra \$2,000 available to us over a period of 12 months, we are more likely to fritter that money away buying stuff at Starbucks or Cabela's than to save or invest it for gain. A lump sum of \$2,000 once a year gets our attention much more strongly.

For many of us without a plan – or the steadfast ability to stick to the plan – it can be smart to let the government hold our money for the year and receive a lump-sum refund at the end. Tax refunds can help taxpayers in key ways, including:

1. **Saving for a big purchase**
   Over the years, our family has used our tax refunds for trips, home repairs, down payments for cars, summer college tuition, a moped, medical bills, and lots of other things. Having that lump sum come in every year was a godsend, especially when we were young and money was tight. As a 20-something young mom I wasn't organized enough to plan our finances just right. Getting a refund served as a forced saving mechanism that helped us out with big expenses come springtime.

2. **Jumpstarting an emergency fund**

   Financial experts agree that everyone should have some money in an emergency fund. Most recommend saving three to six months' worth of expenses in an accessible, liquid account to pay for unexpected events. If you are living paycheck-to-paycheck, it's hard to put any extra money in such a fund. Fortunately, your lump-sum tax refund can fund that account.

3. **Avoiding penalties**

   If you withhold too little tax in a year, you could have to pay an underpayment penalty.[24] Most taxpayers avoid this penalty if they paid at least 90% of the tax due for the current year or 100% of the tax shown on the return for the prior year, whichever is smaller, or if their total tax bill after withholding is less than $1,000. But how many of us check how we're doing on paying tax in the middle of the year? This is impractical for many people.

Other smart moves

Of course, as the experts note, there are very good ways to use the extra money from adjusting your withholdings if you know you can be disciplined about it.

In our low-interest-rate environment, money in liquid savings like savings accounts, money market accounts or CDs doesn't make much for you. If you invest the extra money in the stock market instead, you could see much better returns. However, let's face it, it's unlikely that a relatively small amount in your monthly budget is going right to your Betterment account or your credit card bill.

You could also use the extra funds to pay down your high-interest debt like credit card debt. This is a great move since credit card debt is expensive…but only if you actually use that money to pay extra on your credit card. If not, you'll end up with nothing to show for your extra disposable cash and no refund to count on. If you have credit card debt and you can really commit to using the extra money in our paycheck to pay it down, you will be ahead of the game. If you skip a month here and there…and here…the plan falls apart.

The final word? If you are organized enough to do the no-tax-refund thing right – using the money to pay down debt or invest it – more power to you. If not, don't worry too much about changing your withholding. But, whether it's jumpstarting your emergency fund or making a big purchase, do make smart decisions about how you'll use your lump-sum refund.

WILLS AND ESTATES

Many of us feel as if we will have so little when we die that we don't need to worry about a will. Our modest home, 10-year-old minivan, jon-boat, credit card debt, depleted 401K, and tiny bank account certainly don't constitute an "estate," we think, and it's obvious that all that stuff will just go to our spouse and then onto the children later. In theory, that's true, and in the end the probate court of your home state will eventually distribute your assets to people related to you. It's better, however, to have control of where your assets will go when you die: you'll minimize family heartache and hassle if you take the time to formally state what should happen to your assets after death.

The following three documents should be in every adult's safety deposit box:

- Last Will and Testament
- Health Care Power of Attorney (also called a Health Care Proxy)
- Living Will

The Last Will and Testament is a legal document that states where your financial and physical assets should go when you pass away. Most people use a lawyer to create this document, but you can use online templates or sometimes even hand-write a will yourself. In addition to dispensing your stuff, it also lets you "make charitable bequests; and you can nominate someone in whom you have confidence to be a guardian of your minor children."[25] You want to be the one who has made these important decisions; you don't want to leave it up to random bureaucrats in your state's probate department to decide who will raise your kids and get your assets.

Keep in mind that a will doesn't usually supersede beneficiary designations on life insurance or 401(k) plans, so you want to keep them up to date in addition to having a will.

As explained by the SC Office on Aging, in the Health Care Power of Attorney (also called a Health Care Proxy) "you name an agent who will tell the doctor what treatment should or should not be provided. [It] also should be discussed with the people you intend to name as your agent and alternate agents to make sure that they are willing to serve and know your wishes. The agent named in a health care power of attorney can make the decisions about your health care. [In contrast], a living will only tells the doctor what to do if you are permanently unconscious or if you are terminally ill and close to death. A health care power of attorney is not limited to these situations."[26] A Living Will (or Medical Directive) documents what you want to happen if you are incapacitated and death is imminent or if you are in a persistent vegetative state. Each state has its own specific form to download and complete. The questions on these forms are disturbing, and I can understand why people put off completion of these forms. However, if you are ever in this kind of situation, your family will be glad you overcame your fears and filled it out. In South Carolina, the forms are available from the SC Lieutenant Governor's Office on Aging (see Appendix 3 for website); your state will have a similar site to access forms.

Remarriage and Retirement Issues

It may seem unimaginable when your spouse first dies, but you may at some point want to remarry. Keep in mind that remarriage could have negative financial repercussions with regard to Social Security benefits and pension plans. For example, your Social Security monthly payments could be reduced if you remarry before you turn age 60 because you lose the privilege of claiming based on your deceased spouse's record. If you remarry after age 60, you can collect either on your deceased spouse's record, your new spouse's record after you meet the time requirements, or your own record. It seems an arbitrary age limit for Social Security to set, but you want to be aware of it in case you were to marry a person who has lower lifetime earnings than the deceased spouse did. When he or she reaches retirement age and the spouse is still living, a person is entitled to take either his or her full Social Security amount OR half their spouse's monthly amount, whichever is higher. As a widow or widower, a person gets either their full amount or the deceased spouse's full amount, whichever is higher. (Note: payment amounts go up when a person delays taking Social Security; I discuss these rules more in Chapter 5).

Can You Be Responsible for Your Parents' Debt?

Most parents hope to be able to leave money for their children after they die. What happens, however, if a parent dies in debt? Are their adult children responsible to pay their debts? The answer to this question is "Usually, no." When a person dies, their "estate" (which is the money and property they leave behind) is responsible for their debts. What if the remaining debts are greater than the estate? In the case of "secured debt" where there is collateral like a house, car, or boat, the bank would re-possess the item and write off the loss if any. Unsecured debt such as personal loans, student loans, or credit card debt would go unpaid after the estate is reduced to zero. It's true that in paying the debts money that was to go to heirs would be used up, but the heirs are not responsible for paying that debt out of their own pockets once the deceased person's net worth is gone. If you have co-signed a loan, are listed as an owner on a real estate transaction, are a co-creditor on a credit card, or have in some other way obligated yourself as responsible for the debt, then the debt would be your out-of-pocket responsibility.

It's interesting to note that more than half of U.S. states have "filial responsibility" laws, which are generally old laws on the books from our country's infancy that say adult children are responsible for caring for or financially helping parents who are unable to pay for care. These laws tend not to be enforced, although a case in Pennsylvania did result in a son being required to pay for his mother's nursing home care when she left the country. Other cases have been reported where parents have successfully sued their adult children for support. Additionally, some states with heavy Medicaid long term care expenses are looking at these laws as a possible way to relieve the burden. However, in 2016 it's unlikely that you would need to pay for your parents' care or debt during their lives or after they have died.

CHAPTER 2
ADVANCED FINANCIAL INFORMATION

Once you've got the basics down and are saving money, you'll want to figure out where to put that money so that it can work for you. It's a great feeling when you put $1,000 in an account in January and end up with $1,200 in December, just for having the money sit there. I talked about compound interest in Chapter 1. Interest is money a bank pays you for the privilege of using your money. In 2016, interest rates are low, so money in a low- or no-risk place like a bank doesn't earn very much. In order to earn bigger returns on your money, you want to learn about the different types of investments you can buy, evaluate the risk they carry, and determine what types of investment are best for you.

In this chapter, I'll talk about different types of investments, the risk that can be present in each, and how to determine the level of risk tolerance you might have with regard to investing. I'll also look at how you can manage your own investments and places you can go to get help.

INVESTMENT PRODUCTS

What can you invest in? So many opportunities are out there, but the following list represents the most typical types of vehicles investors turn to.

- *Stocks* – own a piece of the company you invest in. If the company does well, you make money; if it does poorly or closes its doors, you lose money.

- *Bonds* – loan money to the company like a bank would. You get paid interest on this loan over time, but the company will take a negotiated amount of time to pay you back.
- *Certificates of Deposit (CDs)* – invest in a low-risk, low-return savings account for a specified period of time and a known rate of return.
- *Mutual funds* – pool your money with that of other investors to directly buy funds made up of stocks, bonds, and other investments
- *ETFs* – pool your money with that of other investors to directly buy groups of stocks
- *Annuities* – pay a company to hold your money and later they pay you regular payments over time
- *REITs* – pool your money with other investors to invest in large-scale, income-producing real estate
- *Real estate* – own land or buildings that are expected to gain in value
- *Business ownership* – own a company that is expected to gain in value
- *Retirement investments* – use the investment types above to have regular cash flow when you get older and stop working

Stocks (or Equities)

A stock is a share of a company that is sold to the public. Companies sell stocks to raise money to finance business operations. Stock prices change, sometimes by the minute. The stock market is where shares of stock of different companies are bought and sold.

People buy stocks for several reasons including capital appreciation (which occurs when a stock rises in price) and dividends (which are payments made to stockholders when the company distributes some of its earnings to stockholders). As an investment, stocks have produced the highest long-term returns over the past several decades. Investors willing to stick with stocks over long periods of time, say 15 years or more, generally have been rewarded with strong, positive returns. Stocks also have had the biggest swings in performance and are subject to much greater short-term risk of losing money. Of course, just because something happened in the past doesn't mean it will happen again.[27] There is just no guarantee that a person will make money owning stocks.

There are about 8,000 companies whose stock you can buy on two main stock exchanges – the New York Stock Exchange (NYSE) and the NASDAQ Exchange. Stocks can be categorized in many ways. One important way is by comparing the market capitalization (which is basically the size of the firm), which includes large-cap, mid-cap, and small-cap companies. Shares in very small companies are sometimes called "microcap" stocks. The very lowest priced stocks are known as "penny stocks." These companies may have little or no earnings. Penny stocks do not pay dividends and are highly speculative. Stocks are also grouped by how much and how fast the company is likely to grow.[28]

- *Growth stocks* have earnings growing at a faster rate than the market average. They rarely pay dividends and investors buy them in the hope of capital appreciation. A start-up technology company is likely to be a growth stock.
- *Income stocks* pay dividends consistently. Investors buy them for the income they generate. An established utility company is likely to be an income stock.
- *Value stocks* have a low price-to-earnings (PE) ratio, meaning they are cheaper to buy than stocks with a higher PE. Value stocks may be growth or income stocks, and their low PE ratio may reflect the fact that they have fallen out of favor with investors for some reason. People buy value stocks in the hope that the market has overreacted and that the stock's price will rebound.
- *Blue-chip stocks* are shares in large, well-known companies with a solid history of growth. They generally pay dividends.
- *Penny stocks* are the very lowest priced stock of companies with little or no earnings. They pay no dividends. These stocks are high risk and should be avoided. They are also often "illiquid" (hard to sell) because most professional money managers aren't permitted to trade them.[29]

Some companies pay "dividends" to their shareholders. A dividend is cash paid regularly to its shareholders by a company out of its profits or reserves. When you own stock in a company that pays dividends, you receive a cash payment each time dividends are distributed, which for most companies is quarterly. The company sets a rate per share of how much they will pay. For example, in 2016, PNC Bank pays an annual dividend of $2.04 or (51 cents per quarter) for each share you own. That means if you owned 100 shares of PNC, you would be paid $51.00 that quarter (51 cents times 100 shares). You would continue to receive that cash payment each quarter for as long as you owned the shares and as long as PNC chose to continue to pay that dividend. There are many websites that list which company stocks pay dividends, what the dividend amount is, and how often the dividend is paid. See Appendix 3 for a list.

Bonds

A bond is a debt security that is a promise to repay at the end of a specified period. Bonds are issued to raise money from investors willing to lend money for a certain amount of time. When you buy a bond, you lend to the "issuer," which may be a government, municipality, or corporation. In return, the issuer promises to pay you a specified rate of interest during the life of the bond and to repay the principal, also known as face value or par value of the bond, when it "matures" or comes due after a set period of time.[30] People buy bonds for many reasons including their predictable income stream, the offset they provide to stocks, and the return of principal at the end of the prescribed investment period (called the "maturity") of the bond.

The three main types of bonds are corporate bonds, municipal bonds, and government bonds.[31] Corporate bonds are debt securities issued by private and public corporations. You can buy investment-grade bonds with higher credit ratings than those associated with high-yield corporate bonds. High-yield bonds have a lower credit rating than investment-grade bonds and, therefore, offer higher rates of return for the increased risk. Municipal bonds, called "muni's," are debt securities issued by states, cities, counties, and other government entities. Types of municipal bonds include general obligation bonds, revenue bonds, and conduit bonds. Each has different levels of risk. The benefit of a muni bond is that the owners usually don't have to pay Federal (and usually state) tax on the interest they earn. U.S. Treasuries are issued by the U.S. Department of the Treasury on behalf of the Federal government. Types of U.S. Treasury debt include Treasury bills, notes, and bonds of different end dates or "maturities." The "Savings Bond," which is a popular baby present, falls into this category.[32] U.S. Treasury securities are low risk and thus are also relatively low return to compared to other types of bonds.

Certificates of Deposit

A certificate of deposit (CD) is an account that holds a fixed amount of money for a fixed period of time, such as six months, one year, or five years, and in exchange, the issuing bank pays interest. When you cash in or redeem your CD, you receive the money you originally invested plus any interest. Certificates of deposit are considered to be one of the safest savings options; however, it is important to keep in mind that the safer the investment, the lower the return.[33] You are also subject to a 10% penalty if you cash in a CD before its specified maturity date.

Mutual Funds

A mutual fund is a company that pools money from many investors and invests the money in securities such as stocks, bonds, and short-term debt. The combined holdings of the mutual fund are known as its portfolio. Investors buy shares in mutual funds. Each share represents an investor's part ownership in the fund and the income it generates.[34] Mutual funds are very popular among U.S. investors especially for retirement investments such as 401(k)s and IRAs. They are helpful for inexperienced investors because they offer:

- *Professional Management.* The fund managers do the research for you. They select the securities and monitor the performance.
- *Diversification* or "Don't put all your eggs in one basket." Mutual funds typically invest in a range of companies and industries. This helps to lower your risk if one company fails.

43

- *Affordability.* Most mutual funds set a relatively low dollar amount for initial investment and subsequent purchases.
- *Liquidity.* Mutual fund investors can easily redeem their shares at any time for the current net asset value (NAV) plus redemption fees.[35]

Most mutual funds fall into one of four main categories – money market funds, bond funds, stock funds, and target date funds. Each type has different features, risks, and rewards. Money market funds are a type of mutual fund with lower risk and thus lower return. They can invest only in certain high-quality, short-term investments issued by U.S. corporations, and Federal, state and local governments. Bond and stock mutual funds are those which invest in bonds and stocks respectively. Target date or "lifecycle" mutual funds allocate investments based on your planned retirement date.

Exchange-Traded Funds (ETFs)

ETFs are a type of exchange-traded investment product that offers investors a way to pool their money in a fund that makes investments in stocks, bonds, or other assets and, in return, to receive an interest in that investment pool. Unlike mutual funds, however, ETF shares are traded on a national stock exchange.[36] ETFs are not the same thing as mutual funds. Generally, ETFs combine features of a mutual fund, which can be purchased or redeemed at the end of each trading day at its net asset value per share, with the intraday trading feature of a closed-end fund, whose shares trade throughout the trading day at market prices.[37] To put the difference between mutual funds and ETFs in perspective, imagine a day like Black Monday, October 19, 1987 when the stock market dropped 22.6%. If you had owned ETFs (which were actually not sold in 1987), you could have sold your ETF shares at any time during the day for their value at the moment, which was higher as the market was falling than it was when the day ended 22% lower. Had you owned a mutual fund and sold during the day, the brokerage would have taken your order when you said sell, but the sell price would have been calculated at the end of the day based on the net asset value, which in a 22% drop, would have been very low. The ability to sell the ETF immediately for its price right then as opposed to getting the end-of-the-day value for the mutual fund could save money in the event of a rare market crash.

Mutual funds are still the cornerstone investment of many retirement plans, but ETFs have been gaining in popularity in the past few years. Which is a better choice for your investment portfolio? If you are a long-term, buy-and-hold investor with little interest in trading, you are probably fine with highly rated, no-load mutual funds held by a reputable fund manager since the ability to trade often and quickly is not a characteristic that is important to you. If you prefer to buy and sell more frequently, ETFs offer greater tradability, lower costs, diversification, and transparency and therefore may work better for your objectives.

Annuities

People might buy annuities to help manage their income in retirement. Annuities provide three things:

- *Periodic payments for a specific amount of time.* Payments may be for the rest of your life or the life of your spouse or another person.
- *Death benefits.* If you die before you start receiving payments, the person you name as your beneficiary receives a specific payment.
- *Tax-deferred growth.* You pay no taxes on the income and investment gains from your annuity until you withdraw the money.

There are three basic types of annuities: fixed, variable, and indexed.[38] Here is how they work:

- *Fixed annuity.* The insurance company promises you a minimum rate of interest and a fixed amount of periodic payments. Fixed annuities are regulated by state insurance commissioners. Please check with your state insurance commission about the risks and benefits of fixed annuities and to confirm that your insurance broker is registered to sell insurance in your state.
- *Variable annuity.* The insurance company allows you to direct your annuity payments to different investment options. Your payout will vary depending on how much you put in, the rate of return on your investments, and

expenses. The U.S. Securities and Exchange Commission (SEC) regulates variable annuities. A variable annuity is an investment product with insurance features. It allows you to select from a menu of investment choices, typically mutual funds, within the variable annuity and, at a later date – such as retirement – allows you to receive a stream of payments over time. The value of your variable annuity will depend on how your investment choices perform. An annuity is a contract between you and an insurance company that requires the insurer to make payments to you, either immediately or in the future. You buy an annuity by making either a single payment or a series of payments. Similarly, your payout may come either as one lump-sum payment or as a series of payments over time.

- *Indexed annuity.* This annuity combines features of securities and insurance products. The insurance company credits you with a return that is based on a stock market index, such as the Standard & Poor's 500 Index. Indexed annuities are regulated by state insurance commissioners.[3940]

Some people look to annuities to "insure" their retirement and to receive periodic payments once they no longer receive a salary. There are two phases to annuities, the accumulation phase and the payout phase. During the accumulation phase, you make payments that may be split among various investment options. In addition, variable annuities often allow you to put some of your money in an account that pays a fixed rate of interest. During the payout phase, you get your payments back, along with any investment income and gains. You may take the payout in one lump-sum payment or as a regular stream of payments, generally monthly.

All investments carry a level of risk. Make sure you consider the financial strength of the insurance company issuing the annuity. You want to be sure the company will still be around, and financially sound, during your payout phase. Variable annuities have a number of features that you need to understand before you invest. Understand that variable annuities are designed as an investment for long-term goals, such as retirement. They are not suitable for short-term goals because you typically will pay substantial taxes and charges or other penalties if you withdraw your money early. Variable annuities also involve investment risks, just as mutual funds do.[41]

All investments come with fees – they are products sold by companies that need to make a profit on their sales. Annuities are a type of investment with a number of fees you might not be aware of. They include:

- *Surrender charge.* This fee is a penalty for making an early withdrawal above the free withdrawal amount, usually a percentage of the amount withdrawn.
- *Mortality and expense risk charge.* This charge is equal to a certain percentage of your account value, typically about 1.25% per year. This charge pays the issuer for the insurance risk it assumes under the annuity contract. The profit from this charge sometimes is used to pay a commission to the person who sold you the annuity.
- *Administrative fees.* The issuer may charge you for record keeping and other administrative expenses. This may be a flat annual fee or a percentage of your account value.
- *Underlying fund expenses.* In addition to fees charged by the issuer, you will pay fees and expenses for underlying mutual fund investments.
- *Fees and charges for other features.* Additional fees typically apply for special features such as guaranteed minimum income benefits or long-term care insurance. Initial sales loads, fees for transferring part of your account from one investment option to another, and other fees also may apply.
- *Penalties.* If you withdraw money from an annuity before you are age 59½, you may have to pay a 10% tax penalty to the IRS on top of any taxes you owe on the income.

Real Estate Investment Trusts ("REITs")

Real estate investment trusts ("REITs") give you the chance to invest in large-scale, income-producing real estate. A REIT is a company that owns and typically operates real estate like office buildings, shopping malls, campus housing, apartments, hotels, resorts, self-storage facilities, warehouses, and mortgages or loans.

Unlike other real estate companies, a REIT does not develop real estate properties to resell them. Instead, a REIT buys and develops properties primarily to operate them as part of its own investment portfolio. REITs provide a way for individual investors to earn a share of the income produced through commercial real estate ownership without actually having to go out and buy commercial real estate. REITs offer a way to include real estate in your investment portfolio.[42] They let you own small pieces of big-dollar properties. But there are some risks, especially with non-exchange-traded REITs that can be hard to sell when you want to sell them. REITS are susceptible to interest rate rises in that REIT values generally rise as interest rates rise.

Real Estate

Owning a house or land is a financial investment that often results in great financial benefit. It's an exciting day when you finally pay off the mortgage on your main home, and owning the place free and clear gives you a comfortable assurance that at least you've got a place to live no matter how tough things get. A vacation home can be another great investment vehicle if you are able to afford one while still investing for your retirement. A drawback with regard to real estate investments is their lack of "liquidity." In other words, an investment that is not "liquid" is one that is not able to be sold quickly and easily for the same amount you put in to it. You can go to the bank and collect the money you hold there in cash, and you can quickly sell a certificate of deposit – these investments are very liquid. You can also sell a stock easily and quickly, which makes it liquid, but if the stock has decreased in value and you must have the money, you will lock in a loss if you sell at a price lower than you bought it. Real estate is not considered liquid. You may or may not be able to sell a property right away, and the price you get may be far lower than market value or lower than you paid for it. Real estate investments do provide diversification in an investment portfolio.

Owning or Investing in a Business

If you have your own small business or are part-owner in a friend's business, you're making an investment with all the potential rewards and risks that go with it. Business ownership can be a lucrative investment that sets you up financially for life or a devastating mistake that cripples your financial plan. If you own a business, be sure to purchase and keep up the premiums for the kind of insurance best suited to that type of enterprise. Think of your contributions to a business as an investment.

Retirement Investments

All the investment types above can help you prepare for having enough money in retirement. You also will want to take advantage of plans offered that save you in taxes right now in your highest-earning years as you put money away for retirement. Your company or union may offer a 401(k) retirement plan where you contribute (and sometimes the company contributes) tax-deferred money. When you retire and start taking the money out, that's when you pay taxes. If your company doesn't offer a 401(k), you can set up and contribute to your own Individual Retirement Account (IRA). Regardless of what kind of a plan you have, you'll probably invest in stocks, bonds, mutual funds, ETFs, and REITs within that plan. Chapter 5, Retirement, covers more about how to prepare for your retirement years.

RISK AND YOUR "RISK TOLERANCE"

My husband's deer hunting hobby is a good way to illustrate investment risk. He loves to hunt, and he invests a lot of money in the sport. He buys guns, ammo, corn, deer stands, Scent-away, camouflage clothing, licenses, and other items to make it more likely he will get a deer. Then he invests a lot of time driving to hunting grounds and sitting in deer stands. At the end of the deer season, he may have gotten five deer or no deer. He could do all the correct things and spend the right amount of time to see a return on the "principal" he invested in gear and guns, but since he has no guarantee that he will get any deer, he may see little or no return on that investment. He could also lose even more than the principal he invested if he were to fall out of the deer stand, get gored by a feral hog, or drop a gun in the creek.

Investing is similar. You can do the research to find good stocks, buy at a low price, keep up with the market, and follow news related to your stocks, but the economy or problems with the company whose stock you own can make your investment decrease or go to zero. Some investments can even cost you more than your original investment. So you might make lots of money on a stock or exchange traded fund (ETF), you might lose some money, or you might lose all the money you invested. That's the risk you need to be aware of. How do financial professionals define levels of risk? In general, "an aggressive investor, or one with a high risk tolerance, is willing to risk losing money to get potentially better results. A conservative investor, or one with a low risk tolerance, favors investments that maintain his or her original investment."[43] Your risk tolerance level is personal to you; there's no "correct" amount of risk a person should feel compelled to take.

In my husband's case as a deer hunter, the pleasure of hunting makes the cost worthwhile. But most of us invest less for pleasure and more for reasons like paying for college education or for retiring, so losses can hurt badly. When you choose investments, you need to be aware of how much you could possibly lose in that particular investment, acknowledge that you are willing to lose that much, or decide on a level at which you will sell (a "stop loss") so that you don't lose more money than you are able to safely lose.

How does risk tolerance affect your return potential? When you put your money in the bank, it doesn't earn very much for you, but it's safe. When you buy stocks or bonds, you can earn more but you face greater risk of losing the money you've invested. Many investment websites offer free online questionnaires to help you assess your risk tolerance and some estimate asset allocations based on responses to the questionnaires. While the suggested asset allocations may be a useful starting point, keep in mind that the results may be biased towards financial products or services sold by companies sponsoring the websites.[44] To get an idea of your risk tolerance, go online and take an impartial, non-sales-based risk tolerance survey (see links in Appendix 2) to see how much risk you are comfortable in taking. If you can stomach losing some or lots of money, you could choose riskier investments that have the potential to make greater gains. If your risk tolerance level is lower, you'll want to choose safer investments with less return and lower chance of loss. Don't worry - there is no "right" level of risk tolerance; it's just the level that feels right to you. You can find good investments at every risk level.

What if you and your spouse or significant other have vastly different risk tolerances? It's true that "market fluctuations can be unnerving to some investors. A stock's price can be affected by factors inside the company, such as a faulty product, or by events the company has no control over, such as political or market events. Stocks usually are one part of an investor's holdings. For investors who are uncomfortable with the risk or who "just don't want to lose any money," stocks can cause a lot of lost sleep and even more family quarrels.[45] If you two as a couple don't agree on how much risk you are comfortable in taking, it's probably best to keep your finances and investments as separate as possible. It's hard enough to watch a loved one lose money as a result of a market downturn or corporate bankruptcy, but losing your own money is even more painful.

How To Invest

You can find thousands of books on how to invest and many financial advisors who you can hire to direct your investments. You can hire someone to manage investments for you or you can do it yourself by using a "robo-advisor" investment house like Betterment or investing on your own by opening a brokerage account with a place like Etrade, Fidelity or one of the many others out there. For the do-it-yourself approach, I like the safe, un-biased government website http://www.investor.gov to learn about investing in general.

The SEC offers "guiding principles" for investors.[46]

- *Make a Plan* – Figure out where you're starting from financially as discussed in Chapter 1.
- *Save and Invest for the Long Term* – You're not going to get rich overnight, and any investment that promises you that outcome is a trick, as I talk about in Chapter 3. The best protection against risk is time. On any given day the stock market can go up or down. Sometimes a market downturn can last for months or more. Over the years, investors who adopt a "buy and hold" approach to investing tend to come out ahead of those who try to time the market, although people have also made a lot of money in active trading.

- *Investigate Before You Invest* – Do your homework before you part with your money. You can call your state securities regulator to check up on the background of any person or company that you're considering doing business with (see Appendix 7). Find out as much as you can about any company before you invest in it. Companies that issue stock have to give important information to investors in a document called a "prospectus" and by law that information is supposed to be truthful. Always read the prospectus.
- *Don't Wait* – Time can be one of the most important factors determining how much your money will grow. Even if you only have small amounts to invest, do it anyway.
- *Do the Math* – Use financial calculators. Several good ones are listed in Appendix 7.

KEEPING YOUR MONEY SAFE

In any kind of shopping, it can be so hard to know if the product you are being sold is a good deal. Buying investments is a kind of shopping, but in a field where you may not know the terms or the products being offered very well. I'm great at shopping for groceries or clothes; I'm less adept at shopping for power tools or hunting gear. When you compare various types of investments as a layperson, it can be hard to know if you are comparing apples to apples.

Whether you're a first-time investor or have been investing for many years, there are some basic questions you should always ask before you commit your hard-earned money to an investment.

Is the Seller Licensed and Certified?

Investigate the background of anyone promoting investment guidance, even before learning about the opportunity itself. You can read about the qualifications, certifications, disciplinary actions, fees, and investment philosophy of various financial professionals at the websites described extensively in Appendix 7 and below.

The first thing you are checking for at each of the three sites listed below is if your financial professional appears there. If someone representing himself or herself as having a particular designation is not listed, that's a bright red flag. You cannot legally operate as a broker or investment advisor unless you are registered with FINRA or the SEC (which of the two depends on the business circumstances, but the person and the firm must be registered with at least one). A person can be a financial planner without any registration or regulation, but if the CFP® designation is used, the person must appear on the CFP® directory. Call or write the appropriate agency to find out if the missing information is due to an administrative glitch or to the dishonesty of the person you are thinking about hiring. It's hard to imagine that a professional would blatantly lie about their qualifications, but it happens. For example, I wanted to connect with a CFP® professional I saw on LinkedIn. When I pulled up her profile, I saw that she hadn't listed where she'd gone to college, which is unusual on LinkedIn where a person's profile usually lists education and training. CFP® professionals must have college degrees. When I checked the CFP Board directory, she wasn't listed. I called the CFP Board number, and it turns out that she had not earned the CFP® designation but was representing herself as having earned it.

The second check is to Google the financial professional's name. It's unlikely that a person would continue to practice even while under sanctions, indictments, or alleged criminal activities, but it's possible. A search may also reveal behaviors or actions technically unrelated to financial service but that could make you uncomfortable with that person such as domestic violence charges or a DUI. You may also discover that the person is active politically or socially in causes different from those you support and thus might not be a good fit for you. An internet search will also turn up articles, books, or advice-column answers written by the person that can give you an idea of the kind of advice he or she provides.

Next, move on to the harder stuff – visit the official sites provided by the bodies that regulate these professionals. The sections below outline the steps to evaluate each designation.

Researching brokers: Details on a broker's background and qualifications are available for free on FINRA's BrokerCheck website (http://brokercheck.finra.org/). At this website, you can search with a specific broker's name, a specific firm, or zip code to bring up a list of local firms. Once there, choose the "Firm" tab and put in your zip code. A list of firms in your area will come up. You can also search on a specific advisor or firm. Click on a firm, then look to the right to see an orange box that says "Get Details." The page that comes up shows four icons identifying what type of firm, any regulatory or disciplinary disclosures, firm inception date, and registration location(s). Scroll down to an orange rectangular box that says "Download Full Report PDF." That report provides more specific detail on the advisor and/or the firm. You'll be able to see broker's qualifications, work history, and customer complaints. The disclosures section will be the most helpful in evaluating a broker. It provides descriptions of actions the broker or firm has taken that have resulted in complaints. It also shows how these complaints were resolved. Depending on the size of the firm, this report can be long. For example, the report for Merrill Lynch is a formidable 1,528 pages, comprised mostly of complaints and court cases against the firm. On this site, you will see firms listed as "Brokerage Firm" and/or "Investment Advisor Firm." A company can be both or either. A brokerage firm sells investment products based on a suitability standard in contrast to an investment advisory firm that is required as a "fiduciary" to put the clients' interests ahead of their own.

Researching investment advisors/financial advisors/investment advisor representatives: The Investment Adviser Public Disclosure website (http://www.adviserinfo.sec.gov/) provides information about investment advisor firms registered with the SEC and most state-registered investment advisor firms. Once there choose the "Firm" tab, and put in your zip code. A list of firms in your area will come up. You can also search on a specific advisor or firm. Click on a firm, then look at the tab choices on the far left. You'll see "Part 2 Brochures." Click there; open the brochure. This brochure provides important information on the advisor and the company her or she works for. Item 5 in that brochure will say "Fees and Commissions." There you can see how much the advisor charges to manage your money and if there is a minimum investment amount. Many advisors only take on clients who invest over a certain amount (like over $100,000 or more). However, other advisors have a low or no minimum required to invest. Be careful to ascertain that management fees are still reasonable even with a low investment amount. For example, our firm charges 1% regardless of the amount invested up to $250,000; above that amount we charge 0.9%. Other firms may charge, for example, 2% to manage accounts under $100,000 then reduce the management fee for larger accounts. If you want to learn even more about the firm, go back to the main website and on the left section you'll see a tab for the firm's Form ADV – "View ADV by Section." The Form ADV will tell you all kinds of information about the company and its business practices and structure. Item 11, for example, is the Disclosure section where you can see if clients have lodged complaints or lawsuits regarding the firm.

Researching financial planners: Financial planners are not subject to the registration requirements that affect and regulate brokers and investment advisors. Anyone can claim to be a financial planner and charge for advice. The planner doesn't need to have any training, education, degrees, or certifications to call him- or herself a financial planner. This lack of regulation is probably due to the fact that financial planners don't actually manage your money; their job is to work with you to achieve general financial health in all aspects of your financial life including cash flow, budgeting, insurance, risk management, taxes, college planning, retirement, and estate planning. In contrast, a broker or financial advisor directly invests your dollars in various investment vehicles like stocks, bonds, Treasury securities, mutual funds, etc. A financial planner might give you poor advice on your general financial path, but a financial advisor or broker makes decisions that could directly result in your losing money.

Although financial planners have no requirements, one organization certifies, tests, regulates, and supervises financial planners. The CFP® designation is offered by the CFP Board. Go to the CFP Board website (http://www.cfp.net) to make sure that your financial planner is a CFP® professional. Put in your zip code to locate a person or search by name. Each person's name and profile will come up, and you'll be able to see if the planner requires a minimum amount of assets. You can also use this site if you want to report your planner for unethical or fraudulent behavior. Another financial planning designation is offered by the American College. The Chartered Financial Consultant (ChFC) designation requires that candidate take a certain number of financial planning online classes. However, ChFCs are not required to have college degrees or to take a comprehensive board exam.

Although it may be possible that you can find an excellent financial planner with no formal education or certifications, the best advice will probably come from trained financial planners. Most financial planners who are committed to offering their clients optimal service will take the time and expense to formally educate themselves and prove their knowledge by passing difficult exams.

It's time consuming to do all this research, and in the end, you still take a risk in choosing an advisor. After you've completed the research, your best bet is probably to pick the professional you like the best and with whom you feel most comfortable. You'll be spending time together and developing a relationship, so after you verify credentials and past practice, you'll be glad you chose the best fit with regard to personality. These tools can seem a bit overwhelming when you first starting using them, but once you look at a couple of Broker Reports or Part 2 Brochures under an investment advisor's Form ADV, you'll start to see similarities and be able to make informed decisions about who can best serve your needs. See Appendix 7 for more information.

Diversification and Asset Allocation

Asset allocation involves dividing your investments among different assets, such as stocks, bonds, real estate, and cash. The asset allocation decision is a personal one. The allocation that works best for you changes at different times in your life, depending on how long you have to invest and your ability to tolerate risk. Your time horizon (when you need the money) and your risk tolerance determine how you allocate your money among your investments.[47]

Diversification is a strategy that can be summed up as "don't put all your eggs in one basket." One way to diversify is to allocate your investments among different kinds of assets, including real estate. Historically, stocks, bonds, and cash have not moved up and down at the same time. Factors that may cause one asset class to perform poorly may improve returns for another asset class. People invest in various asset classes in the hope that if one is losing money, the others make up for those losses. You'll also be better diversified if you spread your investments within each asset class. That means holding a number of different stocks or bonds, and investing in different industry sectors, such as consumer goods, health care, and technology. That way, if one sector is doing poorly, you can offset it with other holdings in sectors that are doing well. Some investors find it easier to diversify by owning mutual funds. A mutual fund is a company that pools money from many investors and invests the money in stocks, bonds, and other financial products. Mutual funds make it easy for investors to own a small portion of many investments. A total stock market index fund, for example, owns stock in thousands of companies, providing a lot of diversification for one investment.[48] However, you want to keep in mind that just because you own mutual funds doesn't mean you are diversified, especially if the fund focuses on only one industry sector. As you add more investments to your portfolio, you'll likely pay additional fees and expenses, which will lower your investment returns. So you'll need to consider these costs when deciding the best way to diversify your portfolio."[49]

Figuring Out How Well Your Investments Are Doing

How can you figure out how well an investment is doing? One simple, easy way to get an idea of how you are doing is to calculate your ROI. You can do this calculation with any investment you have. You take the amount you made on your investment (the gain) and from it you subtract what you paid for the investment (the cost). Then you divide that amount by the total cost.

ROI = (Gains − Cost)/Cost

So if you buy 100 shares of First Energy stock at $30, your cost is $30 x 100 or $3,000. Then you sell those shares for $35 or $3,500, making a profit of $500. Your simple ROI is ($3,500 - $3,000)/$3,000 or 0.16678, which is a return of 16.67%. However, for a true ROI, you need to take into account the costs involved with buying and selling the stock. Say that you manage your own investments and it costs you $9.95 to buy the stock and $9.95 to sell it. Then your ROI is a little less at 16.07%, calculated as ($3,480.10 − $3,000)/$3,000. The reason we use $3,480.10 here is because we subtract the trading fees from the gain to show what you actually made on the transaction. If you used a broker or advisor, you may have paid $20 to buy and sell the stock and a commission of 0.9% to the broker. In this case, your total trading costs are $67 ($20 + $20 + $27). A 0.9% commission on $3,000 is $27. So from the gain, $3,500, you subtract those costs to get $3,433, or what you actually made on the investment. Your ROI would be ($3,433 − $3,000)/$3,000 or 14.43. How about if you sold the stock at a loss? If you sold your 100 shares for $28, your ROI (without adding in sales costs) would be ($2,800 - $3,000)/$3000 or a loss of 6.67%. Mutual fund and other investment products are more complex and require a more involved ROI calculation, but the fees do still reduce your overall returns.

How about a no-load mutual fund? Your bank or investment company statements will calculate this for you and show you on your statement, but you can practice yourself. You bought shares in a mutual fund for $12,000. It's now worth $18,000. Your simple ROI is ($18,000 - $12,000)/$12,000 or 50%. However, even a no-load mutual fund has expenses. The expense ratio, which is not a simple calculation to do, will reduce your return. The higher the expense ratio, the more your return is affected. In a simple calculation like we're doing, we can't accurately account for expense ratios; however, you can compare expense ratios among funds. A good way to analyze mutual funds is to use the FINRA analyzer tool[50] shown in Appendix 7.

In the two examples above, it seems like the mutual fund made you more money than the stock. However, other factors go into evaluating your ROI: the amount invested and the time you hold the investment.

Amount Invested
It's important to consider other factors when evaluating an investment's return. Making $1,000 on an investment sounds great, but it depends on the amount you invested and the length of time you held it. For example, if you bought land for $150,000 in 2006 and sold it for $151,000 in 2016, that $1,000 profit isn't as

impressive. Sure, you got to use the land (and we're assuming that the $1,000 profit includes all of your costs over the 10 years), but compare that to an investment that tied up less of your money for a shorter period of time.

Say you buy 500 shares of a stock at $30 per share ($15,000 plus trading costs), and in a week it goes up to $32 and change. You sell and get $1,000 after costs. That gain required far less of your money but earned you the same amount. At the same time, you owned the land for 10 years, which tied up money that might have been invested elsewhere for better returns, while the stock only locked up your money for a week. A ratio called the compound annual growth rate (CAGR), a more advanced measure of the return of an investment over time, integrates the time value of money into your rate of return. You'd use a financial calculator to figure this rate out.

Time

How long you hold an investment also factors in to the evaluation of an investment. In the case above, you owned the land for 10 years, which tied up money that may or may not have been invested elsewhere for better returns. The stock only tied up your money for a week. How about the mutual fund discussed above? A 50% return seems pretty good. However, you've held this mutual fund for 20 years, which makes the ROI much less desirable. The CAGR, as discussed above, takes into account the impact of time in the return of an investment and you'd use a financial calculator to figure this rate out. Although the ROI equation is a simple way to compare your investments, you'll want to use financial calculators or rely on a trusted financial advisor for more complex, in-depth calculations.

Understanding fees

Buying and selling stocks and getting professional advice on how to manage your investments will result in fees. Fees are not inherently "bad" or crooked, but you want to make sure that they are reasonable and competitive with those of other similar providers. Fee-based investment advisors change percentage fees based on the amount of money they are managing for you. A direct stock plan or a dividend reinvestment plan may charge you a fee for that service. Brokers who buy and sell stocks for you charge a commission. A discount brokerage charges lower commissions than what you would pay at a full-service brokerage, but in that case you have to research and choose investments by yourself. A full-service brokerage costs more, but the higher commissions pay for investment advice based on that firm's research.[51] Whenever you use professional financial experts, you want to be sure you know how much each service, hour, program, or package costs.

Good Financial Calculators

The ROI equation is a simple and helpful way to compare investment performance. With so many different factors, there is no set number for a good or bad ROI. You'll want to use financial calculators or rely on a trusted financial advisor for more complex, in-depth calculations. Regardless of the methods you use, try to regularly check in with your investments so you can make changes as needed. And remember, returns are just one part of the equation when determining the best investment strategy for you. You can access helpful financial calculators online to figure out where you stand with investments. My favorites are at www. investor.gov and include the tools listed in Appendix 7.[52]

How to Invest Money

So to sum up, here are the three ways to invest:
- On your own (through "robo-advisors" or online brokerages like Vanguard, Etrade, TradeStation, etc.)
- Through a registered investment advisor or broker
- Via IRAs or company 401(k)s

You can buy and sell stocks through:
- A direct stock plan (buying stock right from the company)
- A dividend reinvestment plan (using dividends to buy more stock)
- An online broker like Etrade, Fidelity, TD Ameritrade, etc.
- A stock fund (mutual funds that invest just in stocks)
- "Robo-advisors" like Betterment

Buy Stocks Directly from a Company through a DSPP or DRIP

A way to buy stock directly from a company where you want to own shares is called a direct stock purchase plan (DSPP), which is an investment service that lets you buy stock directly from the company or through its transfer agent. Not all companies offer DSPPs and the plans often have restrictions on when a person can purchase shares. You risk being undiversified when you choose one or a few companies and just buy stock in them, but some investors use this method of investing.

With DSPPs at certain companies, you could buy as little $25 worth of stock at a time without paying money or fees to buy that stock. Some companies have DSPPs they run themselves. In that case, you go to the investor relations section of the company website and follow the instructions. The company may or may not charge a fee to buy stock. One example of this stock purchase plan service is from the Kellogg cereal company. You can get more info about their DSPP on their investor relations website.[53]

Other companies allow you to buy stock directly from them through what's called a "transfer agent." An example of a transfer agent that many companies use is Computershare. Go to Computershare's website[54] and you'll see "Buy Stock Direct." There you'll find a list of all the companies for whom Computershare is the transfer agent, the stock symbols, the minimum amount to invest, and the method to accomplish purchases. If you want to buy stock in a particular company, just check the investor relations section of their website to find out if they run their own DSPP or who their transfer agent is.

I talked about stock dividends earlier in this section - a dividend is cash money paid regularly to its shareholders by a company out of its profits or reserves. When you own stock in a company that pays dividends, you receive a cash payment each time dividends are distributed, which for most companies is quarterly. The company sets a rate per share of how much they will pay. For example, in 2016, PNC Bank pays a dividend of $2.04 per year or (51 cents per quarter) for each share you own. That means if you owned 100 shares of PNC, you would be paid $51.00 that quarter (51 cents times 100 shares). You would continue to receive that cash payment each quarter for as long as you owned the shares and as long as PNC chose to continue to pay that dividend.

In a dividend reinvestment plan (DRIP), you choose to have the cash dividends paid by the company automatically reinvested into additional shares of company stock. If you set up a DRIP, the process becomes automated and usually requires minimal monitoring. An example of a DRIP would be a plan offered by the transfer agent of PNC Bank as shown on its website. [55] If you signed up for that plan, each quarter when a dividend is paid, your share of the dividend ($51 from our example above) would be used to buy more PNC stock instead of being paid to you. No purchase fees are charged in this transaction.

If you feel confident that a particular company is going to continue to do well and you want to be part of that anticipated growth, you could participate in that company's DRIP. As with all investments, you want to regularly evaluate the strength of the company and the place it holds in your portfolio.

Buying Stock or Mutual Funds through an Online Broker
If you want to buy and sell stocks or ETFs on your own, you can set up an account with an online broker. In 2016 there are many reputable brokers you can choose from to buy stocks including Etrade, TradeStation, Fidelity, TD Ameritrade, Charles Schwab, Interactive Brokers, TradeKing, Merrill Edge, Options House, and others. Vanguard, Fidelity, and T. Rowe Price are brokers who specialize in mutual funds. Be sure to comparison shop for the best features, fees, and deals.

Conclusion
As you get ready to invest or as you take more interest in and control over your 401(k), keep in mind that the best guidance and information you can get comes from sources that are not trying to sell you anything. Use government, university-based, or other unbiased books and internet sources like those listed in Appendix 3 to learn more about investing and help your money grow.

CHAPTER 3
WHERE DOES THE MONEY GO?
FINANCIAL TRAPS TO AVOID

I've discussed ways to save and grow your money. What's frustrating is when all that hard work is wasted because mistakes are made. And it's easy to make financial mistakes! Whether you lost $30 because you let your bank balance drop below the minimum or $30,000 because of a crooked financial advisor, losses happen and they hurt emotionally and financially. They happen to wealthy, seasoned investors just as they do to the inexperienced. Look at the Bernie Madoff pyramid scheme where millionaires lost millions – those victims were in the upper echelon of financial knowledge, and yet they still were tricked and lost money. I imagine that it bothers a billionaire to take a loss just as much – or more – as it hurts the rest of us. Let's talk about sketchy financial scenarios you might encounter, discuss common mistakes, and explore ways you can spot and avoid them. In this chapter, we'll talk about:

- What to do when you need cash
- Avoiding fraud and bad guidance
- Finding advisors you trust
- Important documents to keep
- Money fears that can impact finances

WHAT TO DO WHEN YOU NEED CASH
It kind of irritates me when self-help gurus complacently tell you to "eat less; move more"; "spend less; save more"; or "hate less; love more." That "simple" advice is hard to follow. Do they not know how good my buttery cinnamon rolls are, how awesome my

daughter looks with expensive blonde highlights, or how much my nana (who I adore!) can drive me nuts? It is simply NOT that easy to manage desire. It's great that some people have willpower of steel, but I don't. Few of us do. All the best planning and scrimping in the world doesn't stop problems, crises, and plain old desire for something new. As writer Neal Gabler so plainly puts it in his article "The Secret Shame of Middle Class Americans," "Life happens, yes, but [stuff] happens, too – those unexpected expenses that are an unavoidable feature of life. Four-hundred-dollar emergencies are not mere hypotheticals, nor are $2,000 emergencies, nor are … well, pick a number. The fact is that emergencies always arise; they are an intrinsic part of our existence. Financial advisors suggest that we save at least 10 to 15 percent of our income for retirement and against such eventualities. But the primary reason many of us can't save for a rainy day is that we live in an ongoing storm. Every day, it seems, there is some new, unanticipated expense – a stove that won't light, a car that won't start, a dog that limps, a faucet that leaks. And those are only the small things. In a survey of American finances published last year by Pew, 60 percent of respondents said they had suffered some sort of 'economic shock' in the past 12 months—a drop in income, a hospital visit, the loss of a spouse, a major repair. More than half struggled to make ends meet after their most expensive economic emergency. Even 34 percent of the respondents who made more than $100,000 a year said they felt strain as a result of an economic shock."[56] These are sobering words from a nationally famous journalist who himself has felt the anxiety of living paycheck to paycheck. What can you do when the next paycheck doesn't come or when an emergency hits that you can't pay for?

I talked about the emergency fund in Chapter 1, and it's important that you have one. But what if you had one emergency and then another one cropped up before you replenished the fund? What can you do when you need money and don't have it? In reality, your options are pretty limited – you need to bring in more cash through another job, sell what you have, cut bills, or borrow. If you have good credit, home equity, or the ability to get credit cards with temporary 0% balances, borrowing money isn't that hard although it still has accompanying risks and worries. When your credit score is low, getting a loan is tougher.

Chapter 1 discussed compounding interest and how it makes your money work for you. When you borrow money, your dollars work for the lender at a much more efficient and lucrative pace because you will be paying higher interest than you will probably ever earn. If your credit is good and you own a home, you have lower-interest options like home equity loans, lower-interest personal loans, and credit card balance transfers or advances. Loans available to those with impaired credit include higher-interest personal loans (secured and unsecured), payday loans, auto title loans, and peer-to-peer loans, all of which can be expensive. I discuss each of these loan types below.

A "secured loan" means that you put up an asset such as your car or house as collateral for the loan. Rates tend to be lower for secured loans because lenders figure they can sell the house or boat to get back their money if you don't pay the loan back. An unsecured loan is guaranteed only by your promise to pay it back. If you don't pay, lenders will work to get their money back, but, as the saying goes "you can't get blood out of a turnip." So lenders run the risk never getting the money they lent to you back. That's why they charge a higher interest rate on an unsecured loan.

If you borrow using any of the loan methods below, you want to watch out for prepayment penalties, accidental overdraft fees, variable rates, and scam artists in general. Although a home equity loan will have lower interest rates, you should make sure that you aren't paying extra or uncommon fees. In a payday loan, you want to consider the Total Amount Repayable (TAR) in addition to the more familiar Annual Percentage Rate (APR). Loans are often quoted in terms of APR, but the TAR should also be considered. The TAR is the total and complete cost of the loan from your first payment to your last including all initiation, rollover, processing, and other fees.

If you borrow money for almost anything, you'll probably see the acronym "APR" somewhere on the documents. In simple terms, APR means the percent you'll pay in a year to borrow that money. Think about it this way – when you buy any kind of service, you have to pay something for it. Borrowing money is a kind of service, and you have to pay some amount for that service. If you borrow for a house with a home mortgage, the APR (or cost of borrowing) is pretty low – maybe 3%-5% in 2016. On the other hand, if you run a balance on your credit card, you may pay as much as 23% APR in interest and fees – that's much more expensive. And if you get into a payday or title loan that you roll over a few times, your APR can be as much as 396%. You can see the incredible difference you might run into for the same "service" of borrowing $1,000. At 2% APR, you'd pay $20 in a year; at 5%, you'd pay $50; at 22% you'd pay $220; and at 396% you'd pay $3,960. So for the privilege of borrowing $1,000, you might pay between $20 at 2% and $3,960 at 396%. A high APR means that you are paying a lot to borrow money. Sometimes borrowers have no choice but to pay a high APR because they have a poor credit record and the lender is worried about the borrower not being able to repay the loan. When lenders consider borrowers as "high risk," they charge more for lending the money.

To be clear, although the interest rate and APR are usually relatively close, their definitions are slightly different. The **interest rate** is the actual cost for borrowing the money expressed as a percentage rate. The APR includes the cost of borrowing the money and other fees like points, mortgage broker fees, and other charges that you might pay to get the loan. So it is usually higher than the interest rate. Another confusing aspect of the APR is when it is a percentage rate that is quoted to you in weeks or months. In that case, you need to figure out how much you are paying for the year to borrow that money so that you can compare apples to apples in shopping for a loan. If you borrow money from a lender who charges 1% monthly, your APR is actually 12% or 1% interest times 12 months in a year.

You'll be a more confident and value-conscious shopper if you are able to understand the basics of the APR. When you compare rates for getting your hair colored, repairing your car, or taking a guided kayak tour, you make sure you know the exact cost, including any extra fees. When you look into the best place to borrow money, you can use the APR to compare and make the right decision.

Practical Tips for Raising Cash

When push comes to shove and you've got to get some money, one or more of these ideas might help.

- Work paid over-time if it's available at your job.

- Sell things you don't need on eBay or at IWanta, being careful not to get scammed by unscrupulous "buyers." Family and friends may also want to buy things from you.

- Consider asking for a raise at work if you haven't gotten one in a while. They won't fire you for asking, and the most they can say is no. If you work for a union, your wages are set by the project labor agreement, but you might be able to take additional training that moves you from journeyman to foreman.

- Get a part-time, second, or seasonal job - finding one can be hard, though! You might have better luck during the Christmas season when stores do a lot of extra hiring. Look into this tactic in September or October so you don't miss out. Be creative about what you can do. My husband and I are 57 and 54 and throughout our careers we have always had at least two jobs – a main job and one or more on the side. Even if your career is not the type that lends itself to consulting, maybe you could earn some extra money by baby-, dog-, or house-sitting or food service or lawn work. Having a second job brings in more money each month and reduces what you spend on entertainment because more of your hours are taken up by working.

- Cut unnecessary bills. Cutting out cable TV or pedicures technically doesn't generate cash, but it leaves you with more cash at the end of the month. It's hard to give up your favorite shows or an activity that makes you feel good, but if you console yourself with the idea that the sacrifice is temporary, that will help.

- Consider asking a wealthier loved one for help. You might ask for help paying a medical bill or a particularly expensive utility bill rather than ask for cash – sometimes a one-time concrete gift is easier to ask for and to give. Many people who are comfortable financially enjoy helping out loved ones who are in a pinch, but they tend not to offer help for fear of hurting feelings or opening the door to being asked repeatedly for help. It can be hard to ask, but it might be worth trying depending on your circumstances. It might be best to ask for a gift rather than a loan so you don't have repayment hanging over your head, and be sure to include an "out" for the person you're asking if they don't want to or aren't able to help. You could send an email or letter to pave the way before asking verbally. Be honest about how hard it is for you to ask and how fine it is if the person doesn't end up helping. If your request is granted, be sure to say thank you verbally and in writing.

- Apply for assistance if you are qualified to receive it. There's no shame in using food stamps, WIC, free or reduced lunch for the kids at school, or other forms of governmental help. Also consider faith-based help from your church, other churches, food banks, or other religious charities.

When You Have to Borrow

If the tips above don't help and you need to get a loan, what are the best options? The dis-heartening statistics show that 76% of Americans live paycheck to paycheck and 60% have no emergency fund, so you're not alone if you get stuck and need money.[57] As I've discussed above, you want to borrow money at the lowest interest rate possible. The interest rate is the fee you pay for using the lender's money. Even though we are in a very low interest rate environment in 2016, it still costs more to borrow money than you can probably earn when you lend it. In other words, when you need to borrow $10,000, you could pay between 3% and 100%+ depending on the lender you are using. When you "lend" your money (by putting it in a bank, CD, money market account, or bond), you are going to earn somewhere between 0.01% and maybe up to about 5%. That's why financial planners are so insistent on consumers getting rid of credit card debt – it can be as high as a 23% interest rate, which is a very expensive way to borrow money. Your invested money can make you between 0.05% and about 8% on average. But borrowed money simply costs more: home loan rates are about 3%; personal loans about 8%; credit card rates about 15% or more in 2016. Payday and other predatory loans cost even more: the APR for a $100 single-payment payday loan may range from 260.71% to 782.14% on 14 day terms. You can see how easy it is to get into debt and why so many Americans are there. Gabler reports that "only 38 percent of Americans would cover a $1,000 emergency-room visit or $500 car repair with money they'd saved…55 percent of households didn't have enough liquid savings to replace a month's worth of lost income, and [many] were concerned about having enough money to cover everyday expenses."[58]

Where can you borrow money when you need it? Let's discuss each of these places:

- Your home in the form of a home equity loan
- Your home by refinancing
- Auto loan from a bank or car manufacturer
- Personal loan from a bank or credit union
- Personal loan from a friend or relative
- Peer-to-peer loan
- Tax refund loan
- Cash advance from your credit card
- Title loan
- Payday or "check-into-cash" loan
- Pawn shop
- Your 401(k)

Home Equity Loan or Home Equity Line of Credit (HELOC)

A home equity loan is a "loan for a fixed amount of money that is secured by your home. You repay the loan with equal monthly payments over a fixed term, just like your original mortgage. If you don't repay the loan as agreed, your lender can foreclose on your home. The amount that you can borrow usually is limited to 85 percent of the equity in your home. The actual amount of the loan also depends on your income, credit history, and the market value of your home." [59] A home equity line of credit or HELOC lets you borrow up to an approved amount by writing a check. Both loan vehicles use your home as collateral for the loan. This may put your home at risk if your payment is late or you can't make your payment at all. And, if you sell your home, most plans require you to pay off your credit line. These kinds of loans can be good if you own a home with equity in it (which means your loan is less than the value of the home) and you are sure that you'll be able to make the payments. Both of these loans offer tax breaks, and both have fees associated with them. However, the interest rate on these kinds of loans is very low – not far above mortgage rates, which are in the 3% and 4% range in 2016.

Refinancing Your Home

Refinancing can be a better option than a HELOC if you plan to stay in your home for more than 5 years and if you can refinance to an interest rate lower your current rate. When you refinance, you essentially sell your home back to the bank, pay off mortgage number one, then re-buy your home with mortgage number two that has a lower interest rate. Since it is costing you less now to borrow the same amount, you end up with a lower monthly payment.

Many borrowers do a "refi with cash out" in which they finance the remaining amount they owe on the house plus additional cash. For example, if you own a home worth $100,000 that still has $70,000 left on a 5% loan rate mortgage, you could refinance $80,000 at a 3.5% rate and end up with $10,000 in cash and a lower interest rate. The bank allows you to do a refinance with cash out only if you've built up enough equity in your house to stand as collateral if you don't repay your loan. The stakes are pretty high…you can lose your home if you default on this debt. That's why few financial planners recommend that you take out a HELOC to pay off credit card debt or take a lavish vacation. The consequences are too great if life's circumstances turn and make it impossible for you to pay your new monthly mortgage payment.

If you think you might move soon or if your current mortgage rate is already low, a HELOC would probably be a better choice than a refi. Because mother, apple pie, and homeownership are dear to American's hearts, our government structures home mortgages in the most affordable way possible to include tax breaks for original mortgages and subsequent home equity and HELOC loans. Both home equity borrowing strategies allow you to take tax deductions. A refi will likely offer more tax deductions than a HELOC, but that's because it costs more in fees, so the deductions are based on money you've parted with. In general, homeowners refinance to get a lower rate and pay lower monthly payments; however, if you get cash back in addition to your refinance, you could end up with a higher monthly mortgage payment. You don't want to reduce your savings rate – for example, start contributing less to your 401(k) – as a result of a refinance.

If you want to go with a refi, shop around for the best mortgage rates, and don't forget to evaluate the deals at your local credit union. Also, make sure you reduce outstanding credit as much as possible and pay your bills on time in preparation for the application process so that you get the best rate possible.

Although home equity loan and HELOC money can be used for anything, most people use this kind of loan as a way to improve their homes. Be honest with yourself…are these home repairs that you *want* (replace an ugly but functional patio) or that you *need* (repair a leaking roof). Sometimes you have repairs that are necessary and unavoidable, so if you plan to stay in your home for a few more years, a refinance could be the perfect solution. However, you don't want to refinance only to put in a pool that the children quickly outgrow, leaving you floating in loneliness like Puff the Magic Dragon while you scrape up cash to cover your higher payments plus the kids' college or tech school tuition. Try not to put yourself in an unsafe financial position reaching for improvements you just can't afford.

Auto Loan from a Bank or Car Manufacturer
If you want to buy a car, you can get a loan from your bank, credit union, or directly from the auto-maker. An auto loan is a type of secured loan in which the car acts as collateral in case the payments are missed; the interest rates can be somewhat higher than mortgage and HELOC rates although in 2016 those rates are pretty similar. Another low-interest rate phenomenon popular since the 2010's for car purchases is 0 percent or close to 0 percent financing for a particular brand of car. Auto-maker loans can work great if you want that particular vehicle, have good credit, and can make the higher payments since the loan is usually for 3 years rather than 5 years. Be sure to read the fine print on any loan you sign.

Personal Loan from a Bank or Credit Union

Banks or credit unions lend money in the form of a personal loan, which is a type of unsecured loan. Interest rates and fees vary depending on your credit rating and the institution doing the lending. Generally, credit unions, which are local banks owned by members rather than shareholders, offer the best rates, terms, and fees, but it's worth checking local and national banks as well to get the best deal. In 2016, the very lowest personal loan rate for those with the best credit is about 6%, but most people would pay 10% or more for a personal loan.

Personal Loan from a Friend or Relative

Consider asking a loved one for a loan. I talked about ways to ask for a gift earlier in this chapter in the section on raising cash. You can use the same techniques in asking for a loan. This action can be very hard, but I feel as if you never know if you don't ask. People can be extremely generous, and many people really want to help their loved ones in any way possible.

Peer-to-peer Loan

Since 2005, a type of loan called a peer-to-peer or P2P loan has become popular. The potential advantage is that a borrower typically gets a better rate and is more likely to get a loan, even with bad credit, whereas the creditor gets a better return on their money than a bank. Some of the sites that provide this service include Prosper, Lending Club, and Peerform. Until relatively recently, these loans had a personal touch, allowing you to enter the amount you hope to borrow, your reason for borrowing it, and your overall credit status. In the past, you could provide information about what difficulty had befallen you, and lenders with an interest in helping you solve your problem might come forward. Based on the information you enter, the site tells you whether a loan will be available to you and will quote you an approximate interest rate. In 2016 and beyond, P2P lending has become more commercial as institutional lenders have taken over the industry. These lenders are less likely to ask the reasons for the need or to work with you in a personal way. Another innovative funding technique called crowdfunding or crowdsourcing has also become popular. Sites like Kickstarter, Indiegogo, Crowdrise, and GoFundMe offer ways for large groups of people to learn of and help meet an individual's financial need for creative projects, medical expenses, legal expenses, family emergencies, inventions, etc.

Tax Refund Loan

During tax season, between January and April, you can get a loan based on money you expect back in your tax refund. This type of loan is also called a Refund Anticipation Loan (RAL). In addition to the fees and costs associated with this type of loan, if for some reason you don't get the tax refund you expected because of an error that the IRS discovers, you still have to pay back the entire loan. Like payday and title loans, many of the lenders who offer this type of loan charge a high APR.

Cash Advance from your Credit Card

If you have a credit card, you can take a cash loan using part of the credit from that card. You use your credit card at an ATM or a bank just like an ATM card. The difference is that you are borrowing the money, not withdrawing it from your own funds like a debit card, so you have to pay interest on it. The interest rate is at least as high as what your card demands, between 12% and 23% or sometimes higher because usually credit card companies charge a higher rate for cash advances. In addition to the high interest rate, you have to pay a cash advance fee which is usually 2%-5% of the amount of the advance. So if you were to take $300 as a cash advance with a credit card that carries a 4% cash advance fee, you'll have to pay $12 just to get the money, on top of ATM fees and interest. Then you'll be paying whatever rate your credit card charges for cash advances, plus you'll be charged that interest right away...no grace period on cash advances! If you decide to take a cash advance, you'll want to repay it as soon as possible because there is no grace period for payment like you get when you use the card to purchase items on credit.

Title Loan

A car title loan – also known as a pink-slip loan, title pledge, or title pawn – is a small, short-term, high-rate loan that uses the clear title on your vehicle as collateral. Some lenders offer car title loans if you have equity in the vehicle, even without a clear title. These loans typically are for 15 or 30 days and have a triple-digit annual percentage rate (APR) - a much higher interest rate than most forms of credit. Car title loans often are for an amount that is 25 percent to 50 percent of the value of the car. On average, these loans are for $100 to $5,500, but they can be for $10,000 or more from some lenders.[60] To get a car title loan, you'd bring your car, the title, your identification, and sometimes a copy of your car keys. The lender takes the title to your car and returns it to you after you have paid back the loan and interest. You'd want to be sure you know the full dollar amount you'll need to repay and also when the term ends. If you borrow more than you can repay in the term of the loan, you will lose your car.

Payday Loan

In a payday or "check into cash" loan, you write a personal check to the lender for the amount you want to borrow, plus the fee charged for borrowing. The company gives you the amount of the check less the fee and holds the check until the loan is due, usually your next payday. If you continue to "roll over" the loan, you will be charged new fees each time you extend.[61] You'll pay a huge amount of interest if you use this type of loan. For example, say you need to borrow $100 for two weeks. You write a personal check for $115, with $15 as the fee to borrow the money. The check casher or payday lender agrees to hold your check until your next payday. When that day comes around, either the lender deposits the check and you redeem it by paying the $115 in cash, or you roll over the loan and are charged $15 more to extend the financing for 14 more days. The cost of the initial $100 loan is a $15 finance charge and an APR as much as 391 percent. If you roll over the loan three times, the finance charge could climb to $60 to borrow $100.[62] Although this type of loan is so expensive that it really should be avoided, in 2016, payday lenders lend to over 19 million American households – that's about one in six, and these are households in the lower socioeconomic levels of the U.S. It's sad that "one of the great ironies in modern America is that the less money you have, the more you pay to use it."[63] Before you take out a payday loan, review the ideas for raising cash discussed earlier in this chapter in the Practical Tips for Raising Cash section. A payday loan is one of the most predatory types of loans you can take out, and if you can possibly avoid using one, it would be much better for your financial health.

Pawn Shop

If all you need is a small amount of cash – like $100 or $200 – you could take a valuable item to a pawn shop and use it as collateral for a loan. The pawnbroker gives you cash for the item and agrees not to sell it until a certain date. If you bring the money (plus interest) before that date, you get the item back. If not, it gets sold. You won't get the full market value for the item, but you'll get the cash you need. Be sure to keep whatever ticket or note the pawnbroker gives you so that you can get your item back when you are ready to repay the loan.

Your 401(k)

Retirement savings are covered in Chapter 5. If you work for a company that offers a retirement plan called a 401(k) and you've contributed, you may be able to get a loan from that plan. Financial planners strongly advise against borrowing from your retirement account, but it can be an option when you are in a financial jam. Not all plans allow loans, and you may not meet the requirements for a loan. The plan will specify how much you need to have in the account, how long you can borrow the money, and at what rate you borrow. If you leave your job, you will probably have to pay the money back fast, usually within 60 days. This option is not recommended since most Americans don't have enough saved for retirement as it is, but it can be a way to access money at an interest rate lower than some of the options discussed above.

AVOIDING FRAUD AND BAD GUIDANCE

I've lived in the same town for 26 years – gone to the same gym, grocery stores, doctors, shopping mall, etc. with pretty much the same people for all those years. After a while, it's hard not to feel that you know and trust these familiar faces even if you've never spoken to them. It would be relatively easy for one of these peripheral acquaintances to perpetrate some manner of fraud because of my lowered suspicions. I'm also more susceptible to fraud when I'm out of my league in that particular shopping arena. I can identify fair prices and good quality in groceries, hair stylists, or in-home nursing care because I have experience in those areas. I could be much more easily de-frauded or led astray when it comes to auto repairs because I don't know much about cars. To protect myself and my money when I buy products or services, I check potential vendors out by asking others about their work and using online verifications like Angie's List, Yelp, and other reliable places. You can – and should – do the same thing when getting ready to hire a broker, financial advisor, or financial planner by visiting the FINRA Broker Check or IAPD sites as discussed in Chapter 2 and in Appendix 7.

Safe Places to Research
When you do your research, look for unbiased websites, articles, and books. If the U.S. government or agency of the government offers information, you know that they are not trying to sell you anything. Non-profits usually have nothing to gain from connecting with you, so you can feel safe there as well. Check out Appendix 3 for a list of reliable, impartial websites that you can visit and not be sold to.

Five Simple Steps[64]:
The U.S. Consumer Financial Protection Bureau offers five worthwhile steps to take when you are deciding about whether to hire a financial professional and who to choose.

- *Stop* – give yourself time to make the decision. Go physically away and plan to meet or call another day. Blame your reluctance on your spouse or parent.
- *Ask* – ask questions about the costs, the risks, the worst-case scenario. If the person rolls their eyes or makes you feel bad for wanting to understand, go elsewhere.
- *Verify* – double check and comparison shop if possible. If a deal seems too good to be true, it probably is, unfortunately. The product or service is probably a fake, a fraud, a trick, or a stolen item.
- *Estimate* – try to figure out the real cost including the fees and charges and contract terms.
- *Decide* – Buy it! Or thank them and leave if you just don't feel right. Don't worry about hurting their feelings or being embarrassed; it's your money and you don't want to lose it. Keep in mind that most decisions are reversible in the immediate period afterwards when you can change

your mind and get your money back. The person or firm is required to inform you of the duration of "rescission period" for the contract or agreement you are signing.

Common Fraud Tactics

We all know about the Bernie Madoff "Ponzi scheme" scandal, but many other similar crooked schemes exist. As explained by the SEC, "a Ponzi scheme is an investment fraud that involves the payment of purported returns to existing investors from funds contributed by new investors. Ponzi scheme organizers often solicit new investors by promising to invest funds in opportunities claimed to generate high returns with little or no risk. In many Ponzi schemes, the fraudsters focus on attracting new money to make promised payments to earlier-stage investors to create the false appearance that investors are profiting from a legitimate business."[65] The Madoff fraud targeted financially savvy rich people; it's not unrealistic to expect that smaller Ponzi schemes might be aimed at average people.

It can happen anywhere. We had a Ponzi scheme operated by a financial advisor in our little town of 30,000 people. In the town where I practice, a financial advisor moved in, made friends, held swanky events, visited the sick, gave to the poor, established an investment fund, and founded a school…until he was arrested for swindling those "friends" he advised. At his trial, he apologized by saying: "I did love them dearly. My clients were my life. … I just hope they don't lose trust in people."[66] Although my heart goes out to those who lost money because of that advisor, as Paul writes to the Corinthians, "and no marvel; for Satan himself is transformed into an angel of light" (2 Corinthians 11:14). I realize how easy it is to be seduced by a charming person.

Other types of financial fraud continue to plague investors. A few include:

- The "Phantom Riches" Tactic – dangling the prospect of wealth, enticing you with something you want but can't have: "These gas wells are guaranteed to produce $6,800 month in income."

- The "Source Credibility" Tactic – trying to build credibility by claiming to be with a reputable firm or to have a special credential or experience: "Believe me, as a senior vice president of XYZ Firm, I would never sell an investment that doesn't produce."
- The "Social Consensus" Tactic – leading you to believe that other savvy investors have already invested: "This is how _____ got his start. I know it's a lot of money, but I'm in – and so is my mom and half of her church – and it's worth every dime."
- The "Reciprocity" Tactic – offering to do a small favor for you in return for a big favor: "I'll give you a break on my commission if you buy now – half off."
- The "Scarcity" Tactic – creating a false sense of urgency by claiming limited supply: "There are only two units left, so I'd sign today if I were you."[67]

"Educational" Websites and Events with Ulterior Motives

How about a free dinner in exchange for listening to an "educational" seminar? This selling tactic is popular, and although it can at times be safe, it usually comes with a hard sell that is tough to resist. After all, they paid for dinner, right? I come from Mennonite people, and I hate to pass up anything free. Complimentary coffee at Publix? Yes, no matter how weak. Free pen? I realize I have a drawerful at home, but you never know. EVERY sample at Costco? Well, not anything with fish in it. But when someone offers a free dinner at one of the fanciest restaurants in town just for listening to a presentation on retirement planning, I would have to say no. Why? Folks, if any finance- or money-related entity offers free breakfast, lunch, or dinner in return for an "educational seminar," you must say no, even if, as Jane Byrant Quinn writes, "you think you're strong enough to go only for the food."[68] These sales events try to stick you with expensive products and will often not provide accurate information. The people who offer these meals are trained salespeople, and they know the psychological techniques to get you to buy. They may not necessarily be evil or crooked; most have a legal product to sell, but if they are giving a free meal, the product is likely to be overpriced. Quinn goes on to say that "the products they sell might come from reputable companies but are often entirely wrong for someone in your personal situation. If you succumb, count on paying high and hidden costs (these salespeople earn big, big commissions for roping you in). So much for the 'free' lunch." Another temptation is that many of these events are run by young people, and if you are my age, everything young is beautiful. I am much more at risk of parting with my money to help the sales record of an earnest young woman or man like my own daughter or son. Even financial advice at church can sometimes be suspect. If you attend church-related financial seminars, make sure you understand the true costs of the service or product being sold.

Keep in mind that most investment advisors or financial advisors or financial planners offer a free consultation where you can learn all you need to know about their services. Our firm, Wilson David Investment Advisors, offers one or more free meetings for potential clients to get to know us. I also hold free educational seminars at libraries, colleges, and community groups in which sound advice is offered and nothing is for sale; my mission in these sessions is to promote financial literacy and is separate from my business.

Too Good to Be True

If something seems too good to be true, it probably is, especially when it comes to financial return on investment. Although a few people may have the luck to score a windfall, most investors make about the same amount from their money based on the risk level of the investment vehicle they choose. Basically, the safer the investment, the less money you will make. U.S. government bonds are almost risk free, and that's why you only make about 1% when you invest in them. You have no guarantees in investing: a corporate bond or biotech stock could give you a 50% return – or the company might go out of business and you would earn no return AND lose the entire amount of principal you invested. A good guideline is to compare your returns with the general accepted returns that comparative investments are making. The New York District Court documents on the Bernie Madoff scandal point out that in the Madoff case, the "the investment performance achieved by [the Madoff Securities] funds…is so consistently and significantly ahead of its peers year-on-year, even in the prevailing market conditions, as to appear to good to be true – meaning that it probably is."[69] In the Madoff case, his clients were earning a steady return on their investment that was consistently far above what other similar investments were making – that's a classic red flag. The Ponzi scheme Madoff ran was fake, and when it collapsed, his clients lost the money they had invested with him.

Secrecy and Hurrying

Almost any (and probably every!) investment opportunity that requires you to buy it right that minute should be avoided. Few of us are in the high-net-worth, fast-breaking opportunity world where a rare, lucrative, quick-turnaround, valid investment vehicle might be offered to us. Even those who are in that category should be wary because few – if any – reasonable financial decisions need to be made immediately. Always take your time to ask questions, think things over, and read the fine print about an investment you might buy.

Also avoid any investment that is a "secret" or is "just for you." Forensic accountant Tracy Coenen explains that "every long-term fraud scheme lives and dies by the secrecy of those who participate…Anyone running a legitimately successful business doesn't have a code of silence. They might not be seeking publicity, but they certainly aren't going to forbid their clients to talk about how successful they are. When an investor is prohibited from talking about the investment, any reasonable person should know something is amiss."[70] Coenen is referring specifically to the Madoff case, but her advice applies to any investment you are considering. If you aren't allowed to tell others about it, can't find information about it easily on the internet, and see no public ads, stay away. Your state securities agency can help here, too – contact them if you have questions about a particular offering.

Go Slow, Especially During a Crisis

When your life is in an upheaval, you want to be even more cautious and slow to act. If a loved one has died, you've lost your job, your town has been hit by a natural disaster, you're going through a divorce, or any other stressful situation is occurring in your life, you need to make decisions slowly, realizing that this is a stressful and uncertain time. Although valid, special, fast-moving deals may be offered to the extremely wealthy with great connections, it's unlikely – and probably impossible – that a lucrative deal that requires a quick decision will be offered to regular old you and me. When you are pressured to make a fast decision because the offer "is only good for today" or "has a limited number of opportunities," you need to stop, dig in your heels, say no, and walk away. If you can find an advocate – a close family member or trusted professional – to help you with truly urgent matters, such as meeting tax or financial reporting deadlines, that will go a long way toward keeping you financially safe. It's inevitable that life will bring us heartache and trouble, but we don't want to add to it by making hurried financial decisions in the wake of a tragedy.

FINDING ADVISORS YOU TRUST

How can you find a financial advisor or planner who you can trust? Unfortunately, there are no fool-proof ways to guarantee honesty. Even so, you can do your homework to make sure you avoid advisors who have already behaved in unethical or criminal ways, and you can get references to see what current clients – and prior clients – think about that financial professional. See Appendix 7 for specific steps to evaluate people who you might hire.

Check Credentials

A first start is to directly ask your financial professional if he or she is a fiduciary. The U.S. Department of Labor's definition of a fiduciary specifies that financial professionals adhering to a fiduciary standard "act in their customers' best interest; adopt procedures reasonably designed to detect potential conflicts; eliminate those conflicts of interest whenever possible; adopt written supervisory procedures reasonably designed to ensure that any remaining conflicts, such as differential compensation; do not encourage financial advisers to provide any service or recommend any product that is not in the customer's best interest; obtain retail customer consent to any conflict of interest related to recommendations or services provided; and provide retail customers with disclosure in plain English concerning recommendations and services provided, the products offered and all related fees and expenses."[71] Consider hiring an financial advisor who is a fiduciary so that it is more likely that your interests will come first, resulting in a better financial outcome for you.

Read the Paperwork

You know you are supposed to read the fine print, but how many of us take the time to really do so? Do your best to try to read and understand what you are signing. Don't leave blanks in the forms you fill out that someone else could complete later without your knowledge or consent – write "N/A" for "non-applicable" in blank areas of importance. Be sure to get hard copies of the final, submitted documents. If you're not comfortable on the internet or don't have a printer, ask for hard copies of documents. Even if there's a charge for hard copy documents, it may be worth paying for them to be sent to you.

Third Party Confirmation

Make sure you receive regular statements from independent third party sources. Usually, these sources are the custodians of your assets – either a brokerage firm or a trust company. Reconcile the statements with reports you receive from your financial professional and ask about any discrepancies. Even printed statements don't necessarily guarantee safety although ensuring that statements come from an independent third party rather than from the advisor's own firm offer added security. In the case of the Madoff scandal and with my hometown Aiken financial advisor fraud event, clients received paper statements regularly that falsely confirmed their accounts were doing well.

Gut Feelings

It would be great if you could count on your "gut" to tell when to buy and when to run. However, gut feelings work best when you are in an environment where you are an expert. I cook a lot, so when my gut feeling says that the water is too cool to make my bread rise properly, I'm right. I'm less of an expert on car maintenance, so that funny sound in my Toyota could mean my coat sleeve is hanging out the door or that the transmission is going. When you don't know much about financial matters, it's harder to judge the competence and honesty of a potential advisor. I do think that if you don't *like* the person or if you have a general sense of distrust, you'd do well to choose someone else, but the reverse isn't necessarily true: plenty of us have made the mistake of liking people who later betrayed us.

What types of advisors have the greatest potential for conflicts of interest and bad advice? Paladin Investor Resources suggests consumer avoid advisors who are:

- Employees of companies that determine what investment types will be sold to investors, such as brand name firms with their own investment products
- Paid with commissions, not fees
- Securities licensed, but are not Registered Investment Advisors or Investment Advisor Representatives
- Not acknowledged fiduciaries
- Don't document credentials, ethics, or business practices[72]

How about if you think you are being cheated? Would you tell people about it? Many don't. The Federal Deposit Insurance Corporation theorizes, in their consumer report, that shame, embarrassment, denial, and self-blame are contributing factors to non-reporting.[73] If you aren't sure about an investment you might buy or have already bought, call one of the government agencies listed in Appendix 7. They'll help.

Checks and Balances

It can be tedious, but make a point to look at your financial statements regularly. If you already own a particular investment, read your paper statements and regularly access your statements online. Financial journalist Jack Waymire cautions consumers that they should "receive monthly, quarterly, year-to-date and annual reports that document your performance. The report should provide performance data that is gross and net of all fees so you can see the impact of expenses on your results."[74] I have to admit that I am the worst about checking all my statements from various places now that they are online and I have to pull them and print them myself. Most banks and investment houses charge a fee now for paper delivery, so I need to get in the habit of downloading, printing, and reviewing all my statements regularly like I used to do when they came in the mail. If you can have paper statements delivered to you without a fee, choose that option.

The Fiduciary Standard

I've used the term "fiduciary" here and briefly defined its characteristics above. Why is the term important to you? Since a fiduciary is a professional who has been charged to manage assets for your benefit as the client rather than for his or her own profit, you are less likely to be offered products based on the commission the financial professional will earn rather than what is best for you. The Certified Financial Planner (CFP) Board considers a fiduciary to be one who acts in utmost good faith, in a manner he or she reasonably believes to be in the best interest of the client. These are legal definitions that bind the advisor to act in your best interests, not his or her own, and if the advisor fails to do so, he or she is liable for civil and potentially criminal penalties. Fiduciaries still might offer you investment products that benefit them more than you, but it is illegal for them to do so – unlike broker/dealers who can legally profit from investments they sell that are not right for you as long as they adhere to a relatively vague "suitability standard" in what they try to sell you. If your advisory is not a fiduciary, ask about the fees associated with the investment being recommended, how those fees compare with other investments, and if he or she will earn a commission if you choose the investment.

With the Possibility of High Returns, Risk is ALWAYS Present

Think of all the weight loss programs and pills out there. If any of the easy ones really worked, we'd all use them and we'd all be slim. You basically just have to eat fewer calories than you burn off, which is really hard to do. It's a fact that the average human body burns a certain amount of calories and nothing safe will let you eat huge quantities and stay slim. Amphetamines or the HIV virus may slim you, but at a huge cost to your physical health. It's the same with financial health. For a low amount of risk, you're only going to be able to make so much money. With short-term CDs, that return is about 0.075% in 2016; with long-term participation in the stock market, the average return over a lifetime has conventionally been figured at about 8%-10% (although experts are beginning to revise that figure down to about 6%-8%). So, if you're offered an investment that's guaranteed to make you a 40% return, the risk is high that you won't make that amount and you could lose your principal. Although you *could* make a 40% or better return, there's no guarantee that you *will* make that much; the risk inherent in the possibility of high returns means that there is a chance you will make less money, lose some of your money, or lose it all.

Realize That Financial Transactions Have Costs Just Like Other Shopping

Whenever you are presented with a proposed transaction, ask "What does this cost me?" Ask about selling costs, surrender charges, loads, commissions, admin expenses, and other transaction charges. It's not wrong or illegal for charges to exist; however, it is unethical (and in many cases illegal) to hide or to neglect to reveal them. It's fine to ask your financial professional if he or she gets paid from the transaction. Third-party payments or commissions aren't red flags all by themselves, but if the benefits aren't enough to make the commissions worthwhile, look for other investment options. Ethical financial professionals always work in their clients' best interests when making investment recommendations. In contrast, unscrupulous professionals may base their suggestions on the size of their commission or fee. If the firm you use is constantly urging you to buy and sell (an illegal practice called "churning"), you may want to go elsewhere. Remember that just because you pay nothing out of pocket doesn't mean that the investment is free.

Speak Up When You Don't Understand

Tell your financial professional when you don't understand; ethical professionals will be happy to explain. If you still don't get the explanation, ask the financial professional to put it in more simple terms. You can also research the investment or concept on your own and present your advisor with your findings as a way to get a conversation started about a transaction you're worried about.

Don't Confuse Familiarity with Trust

When you live in a small town like I do, you get to know a lot of people and you tend to feel very connected and trusting. It's great to ask friends and acquaintances for recommendations about who they trust in the financial world. You just want to make sure that the person you end up choosing is qualified to advise you. You might have a lot in common with the person recommended to you, but you need to run the same verification checks discussed in Appendix 7 on a mutual friend that you would run on a stranger.

IMPORTANT DOCUMENTS TO KEEP

A key component of financial safety is being able to access vital personal information and documentation. What documents should you keep at minimum?

- Birth, adoption, marriage, and death certificates and SSN cards (and copies which you should keep in a different location in your house)
- Passports and passcards (and copies kept in a different location in your house)
- Retirement planning documents (workplace retirement plan, Summary Plan Description)
- Social Security retirement benefits estimate
- Tax planning and tax return documents (tax returns for last year; paystubs; W-2's)
- Financial- and investment-related documents and statements (bank accounts, mutual funds, brokerage, stocks, bonds held, business agreements)
- Loan documents, statements, and credit reports (student loans, mortgage, car, credit card numbers and info, recent credit report)
- Insurance documents and statements (health, disability, long term care insurance, life, homeowners, renters, auto, umbrella insurance policies, etc.)

Many people don't have printers at home anymore, so it's hard to generate the hard copies you need to have to protect yourself. It's worth the money to put statements on a thumb drive and take it to print at the library or Staples. Turn paper statements **on** if there's no charge to have them mailed and be sure to file them where you can access them later. If you don't get paper statements, commit to printing out important items and statements periodically, if not every month. At the very least, record in writing all account numbers, access numbers, contact info, and codes, and keep them in a safe place. You might also want to scan these documents to a thumb drive that you keep in a fireproof box in your house.

MONEY MONSTERS THAT KEEP US UP AT NIGHT

In our discussion of financial traps that can snag you, it's worth talking about the fear and worry with respect to money that can affect our financial decisions. A sense of real panic can be tied up with money matters, especially if you don't understand basic concepts relating to money. Knowledge is power, so the more you know, the less scared you will be. If you have children – or a lasting memory of your own childhood – you understand a child's fear of monsters under the bed. Money monsters terrorize grownups just as much as vampires scare 5-year-olds. Why are we so anxious about the concept of money? And how can we calm our fears?

Monsters are big. Kids are little, and monsters are big. Our paychecks are little, and our bills are big. Being small in the face of a towering troll is frightening, and money worries can easily take the form of a gigantic monster. We carry a lot of mental baggage with regard to money: it can mean joy, sorrow, power, lack of control and so much more than simple dollars and cents.

Monsters might hurt you. Kids don't know what a monster might do to them, and a strong imagination magnifies the terror. Adults are no different when it comes to scary money monsters, especially when they lurch your way clothed in unfamiliar jargon. A bad investment can hurt you, and that's a real terror. You don't always know if a financial decision will turn out to be a fiend or a friend.

Monsters pop out unexpectedly. Kids lie in dread for the moment the monster finally jumps out. Grownups wait in fear of the blindside of the car accident, the health crisis, the stock market drop, or other potential catastrophe, not knowing when disaster might strike. The uncertainty – just like anticipating pain in the dentist's chair – makes life uncomfortable.

Monsters can sometimes be real. Unfortunately, actual scary things can happen to kids at night. Children can't be protected from all danger, and neither can your pocketbook. Tornados tear off roofs. Life-threatening cancers develop. And, as the well-known billboard bluntly shows, when your teenager drove drunk and "just blew $10,000," it's your financial dragon to slay.

How can you ease your money fears?

- *Turn a problem into an opportunity.* Continually being short of cash can be the impetus for you to train for a new job. High car insurance bills might make you a safer driver. Worries about paying for health care in old age could be the reason you stop smoking. Actions you take to reduce fear can impact your life in positive ways.

- *Acknowledge and draw out fears.* Just saying "I'm scared" can start the process of feeling better. Admitting the power money has over us can start us on a path of greater control.

- *Track the trigger.* Often it's just one thing that's really terrifying you – like paying for your kids' college or tech training. In that case, doing your research and nailing down the worst case scenario can minimize the T-Rex looming over you.

- *Tell the truth.* Ignoring money issues won't make them go away. On good days try to face the money ogre, take stock of your financial situation, make plans, and try to stick to them.

- *Create a less scary environment.* Try to be realistic about what you owe. Making a list or putting together a spreadsheet can show the facts, which are often less dire than what you imagine. Make your list after dawn, because realism usually doesn't work when you've seen every half-hour on the clock since 1 am. In the light of day you can take the time to honestly ask yourself if things are as bad as they seemed under the covers last night.

- *Change false perceptions and beliefs.* Many fears are just plain silly. Social Security is highly unlikely to disappear. You're not going to end up a bag lady digging through dumpsters. Being wealthy doesn't make you a bad person. It can be a habit to cling to unrealistic beliefs, but you'll feel better if you can manage to rid your mental landscape of unrealistic fears. I'm personally guilty of this practice, but I continually work to keep my worries in perspective, to avoid "going global" about relatively small anxieties, and to try to be realistic about the worst that can happen.

Don't feel bad if you are reluctant to talk about the money monsters disturbing your sleep. You are not alone: Americans would rather discuss their personal ideas about death, politics, sex, or religion more than they want to talk about private money-related matters, statistics show.[75] We hide our fears about our debt, taxes, net worth, retirement, and many other financial matters. We all know that monsters lurk in the shadows and disappear when light shines on them; try some of these ideas to banish your own money monsters.

CHAPTER 4
COLLEGE AND TECH TRAINING

Many Americans assume that getting a college education is the only path to success. If your child is able to get into college, it is a given that he or she should go. We tend to think of a college degree as the ticket to higher-paying jobs and better lives. A college degree certainly may lead to a great career, but it isn't a guarantee. For example, a blue collar career as a trained ironworker will earn you far more over a lifetime than a career as a college-educated schoolteacher. Let's take a look at the trade-offs between going to college and choosing a different track including:

- The benefits of a blue collar career
- The disadvantages of blue collar work
- Training and preparation for blue collar jobs
- Saving for and paying for college

BENEFITS OF A BLUE COLLAR CAREER

Graduating from college is a worthwhile accomplishment, but it is not an assurance that you'll end up with a high-paying job. Why not? Let's take a look at pay, hours, debt, lifetime earnings, and personal interests in the context of getting a college degree.

Is it necessary for a person to graduate from a 4-year traditional college to progress in the workforce? Certainly, many people with college educations go on to lucrative careers in which they earn high salaries. However, many other graduates are unable to find good-paying jobs – or sometimes any job – because their degree in history or film or fine arts doesn't qualify them to be hired at jobs that pay well. Additionally, college students who major in subjects like education or social work consign themselves to lower lifetime salaries since those jobs pay lower salaries.

Matthew B. Crawford, author of *Shop Class as Soulcraft: An Inquiry into the Value of Work*, in his recent article "Learn a Trade," writes that "we often hear that those with four-year degrees earn more than those without. In fact, they earn a lot more - on average. But these categories are misleading. If you compare the earnings of a diesel mechanic working on heavy equipment in the North Dakota oil fields to those of a person with a degree in sociology working in retail (as such scholars often do), you'll get a very different picture. The mechanic is likely earning about three times as much. Not only is he likely to be making more money, he's almost certainly exercising his intellectual capacities more intensely at work. If diagnosing machines could be reduced to simply following rules, that mechanic would not be earning $100,000 a year."[76] The disparity between white- and blue collar earnings can be substantial, which is why it's important to consider the career path of blue collar employment.

Many blue collar jobs have similarly high pay-scales. For example, from a January 2016 article in *Comstock's* magazine entitled "The Endangered Blue-Collar Worker": "'those who get certified to fix heating and air-conditioning systems make near six figures within five or six years,' says Jon Zeh, chair of the Mechanical Electrical Technology Department at Sacramento City College. 'And they can get that training in a program that offers a 2-year degree for less than $3,500 – or for low-income students, nothing at all. Contrast that with the average $37,000 tuition for an in-state bachelor's degree at California's public universities.'"[77] Another recent example of great pay potential emerged at the Caterpillar Inc. Large Engine Center in Lafayette, Indiana, where a new campaign called 'Advancing Manufacturing: We Have Jobs Here, We Have Training Here' was introduced to promote training for manufacturing jobs including machine operators, production workers, crane operators, maintenance personnel, welders, extrusion technicians, and metal fabricators."[78] It's time to take a second look at conventional wisdom that says college is the only path for career happiness and financial success.

Pay Rates

As discussed above, many jobs that require a college degree don't pay well. Teachers, bank professionals, social workers, human resource analysts, lab workers, and other professionals have important jobs, but our society is not willing to pay high salaries for those particular skills. Many reasons may cause the lower rates including high competition for those jobs, a glut of workers with those skills, a profession dominated by female workers where salaries tend to be lower, or jobs with flexible hours. Regardless of the reasons, if you go for a degree that qualifies you for one of those jobs, you will not be able to earn much more than the average for that sector no matter how talented you are. An elementary school teacher today will not likely ever make $170,000 per year in his or her profession.

Representative annual salaries for jobs that require a college degree include:

- Teacher in South Carolina – $26,000 ($12.50/hour)
- Communications consultant – $32,000 ($15.38/hour)
- Business analyst (master's degree required) – $45,000 ($21.63/hour)
- Human resources manager ($45,500) – ($21.87/hour)

Those salaries are not that great. When you consider that these employees also have college loan debt, which averages about $35,000 per student in 2016, it can be hard to make ends meet and even harder to get ahead as an employee in many white collar professions. Data published by the Board of Governors of the U.S. Federal Reserve show that the millennial generation earns less today after adjusting for inflation that their peers did in the past.[79] Lower earnings coupled with student loan debt make life even harder. In the light of this sobering data, it makes sense for a high school student who isn't sure what he or she wants to do for a career and who really isn't interested in getting a 4-year college degree to take a look at other career options.

I listed sample salaries for typical blue collar jobs in Chapter 1, and many of them far exceed the salaries of some jobs that require a college degree. As explained in the U.S. Chamber of Commerce

Foundation's "Enterprising States 2014" report, "the imperative now is to get people to reconsider their educational options. 'People go to college not because they want to but because their parents tell them that's the thing to do,' observes [Jeff] Kirk [manager of Kaiser Aluminums Heath, Ohio plant]. 'Kids need to become aware of the reality that much of what they learn in school is not really needed in the workplace. They don't realize a pipefitter makes three times as much as a social worker.'"[80] It's interesting to note how difficult the job search can be for millennials with college degrees but no specific, saleable skills: in 2011, more than half of college grads (53.6 percent, 1.5 million grads) under age 25 were unemployed or underemployed, according to an analysis of Current Population Survey data by Northeastern University and research from Drexel University economist Paul Harrington. [81]

Overtime Hours

In addition to the relatively low wages these types of salaried jobs provide, overtime is usually unpaid, which drives the effective wage even lower. For example, if you work 50 hours per week as a communications consultant with a salary of $32,000 (or $15.38 for a 40-hour week), you get the same salary as if you work a normal 40 hours. That means you actually earn $12.30 per hour rather than $15.38. Bosses at most professional jobs expect their workers to put in unpaid overtime. You could refuse, but it's likely you'll be replaced by another eager, unemployed college grad willing to earn $12 an hour. When you work in most blue collar fields, you get paid for your overtime, often at a time-and-a-half rate.

Debt

According to the U.S. Bureau of Labor Statistics, "in the last few years, student loan debt has hovered around the $1 trillion mark, becoming the second-largest consumer obligation after mortgages and invoking parallels with the housing bubble that precipitated the 2007–2009 recession…the proportion of the U.S. population with student loans increased from about 7 percent in 2003 to about 15 percent in 2012; in addition, over the same period, the average student loan debt for a 40-year-old borrower almost doubled, reaching a level of more than $30,000."[82] Grad students incur even more debt, and the salaries, especially in education, aren't usually high enough to make that master's degree (which is a great *academic* boost) a worthwhile return on investment *financially*. If it turns out that college isn't for you or if problems prevent you from graduating, you can end up with lots of debt and no degree to show for it. Having hours toward college doesn't qualify you for a job that requires a degree, so you could end up with the debt and without the necessary letters behind your name. In contrast, blue collar training requires fewer years and costs less than a college degree; in some fields, you learn on the job while being paid.

The Most You Can Make in a Lifetime

Additionally, many of these professional jobs have relatively low caps on how much an employee can ever make. Most professions have customary top limits on the amount an experienced worker is likely to make after a long, successful career, but the limits for a lawyer, doctor, or computer scientist – that only the most elite and specifically trained college grads nab – dwarf the limits for reporters, museum curators, most of those employed in religious good works, rehab counselors, radio announcers, recreational workers, legislators in local government, marriage counselors, historians, social workers, and biological technicians. It's not that these lower-paid jobs aren't important, but the fact is that they just don't pay very much at the beginning of your career or at the end. When you become a museum curator, you're consigning yourself to a life of relative poverty. If you've got student loans to pay off as well, it might not be a comfortable way to live.

When you consistently earn a lower salary, you make less over the course of your career. For example, a guidance counselor's median salary is about $43,000, which works out to about $2.4M over a lifetime career. An ironworker making about $72,000 per year could earn about $4M. Such a dramatic swing in lifetime earnings is enough to make you consider options other than college.

Following Your Passion

As discussed in Chapter 1, Americans don't really like to talk about money. Money certainly isn't everything, and it doesn't buy happiness. However, it's an essential part of living, and without enough of it, life can be very hard and somewhat limited. We need to consider the facts when we choose a career or guide our young people toward career choices. If you feel called to do a certain job, please ignore the following advice. You know what you want to do, and you should do it. In my case, I knew early on what I liked – I loved to write and to teach other people things. At kindergarten age and beyond, I kept diaries and made my sister and my friends play school. I found myself committed to being both a teacher and student throughout my life. I loved going to school and still do. But in choosing teaching and writing, I initially consigned myself to lower salaries until I morphed my skills into business development and then into the financial field. I found that, as I got older, I felt frustrated that I wasn't able to earn higher salaries by teaching or writing. If a passion for history or the environment or God can carry you through a financially restricted life, you're all set. The problem might come in middle age if you have children, become disabled, or find your passion waning. At that point, it's hard and expensive to change careers.

If you feel called to teach kindergarteners, serve God, or save whales, you should follow that passion and get the college degree you need. But what about the many students who feel no such passion yet are under pressure to go to college? Should they just go to college and hope they will figure out what to do for a career? In some cases, the answer is yes. In others - such as when a student has little interest in academics – a better answer, at least financially, is no.

Many – or Few – Compelling Interests
What if you aren't particularly interested in any one thing? What if you like lots of things, but none more than others? What if you just want a job that's a job – one that will allow you to live a great life but doesn't necessarily inspire your passion? I get a little tired of all the "follow your passion" advice that's out there now. Most of us will spend huge amounts of time doing jobs that aren't worth our passion. I don't expect the ironworker tying the 6,000th piece of rebar, the accountant creating yet another balance sheet, or the nurse dispensing meds on the Alzheimer's ward to be constantly passionate about what they do. Hopefully they have a general sense of the value of their contributions to the efficiency of the world as they build a high-level waste tank or enhance the quality of life for the elderly, but much of their daily existence is pretty uninspiring. To tell our young people that they can be passionate about their

jobs every day does them a disservice. Even famous actors or athletes have tedious parts of their jobs – learning lines; running pass routes – that probably get boring.

The boredom that stereotypical thinking attributes to blue collar work is not necessarily accurate. Blue collar advocate Jeff Torlina touts the importance of repetition: "Another misconception of intellectuals is that repetitive work is simplistic and mindless. What is misunderstood is that skill is a product of repetition. Any artist must practice until the art form becomes almost natural. The only way a mason can learn to put a perfect finish on a concrete floor or to build a block wall that is perfectly plumb, straight, level, and consistently laid is to have performed those tasks thousands of times. With repetition comes a feel for the movement that directs the muscles to apply the correct pressure on the trowel or to hold the tool at the proper angle."[83]

DISADVANTAGES OF BLUE COLLAR WORK

Keep in mind, however, that blue collar work is not without problems. It's worth considering possible negative aspects of blue collar work. Six come to mind:

- Irregular pay schedules
- Economic shifts that cause unemployment
- Temporary work in blue collar employment
- Physical danger and wear and tear on the body
- Shortened career duration
- Societal attitudes toward blue collar work

Pay Day

A number of blue collar jobs, especially those in construction, oil and gas, and landscaping depend on good weather. As a blue collar worker, you are usually considered "non-exempt" for human resources and pay purposes. That means you only get paid when you work, in contrast with a salaried worker who receives an agreed-upon amount every week regardless of how many hours he or she actually works. So when it rains, you don't go to work and you don't get paid. A rainy November during a concrete tank construction project can put a huge dent in your wallet and make the kids doubt Santa exists. In addition, in construction, timbering, and other fields, the whole purpose of the project is to work yourself and the rest of the team out of a job. When the tank is built or the forest is cleared, you're out of work until you get on with the next project. Many, although not all, salaried people are kept by the company in between projects, but blue collar workers are laid off, leaving you to collect meager unemployment checks until you're off the bench for the next project.

Changes in the Economy

Economic shifts can negatively affect blue collar workers. In the summer of 2015, the oil industry experienced a huge shake up. Oil, which was at $80 a barrel only a year ago, had gotten as low as $27 a barrel. Oil stocks dropped and companies that produced oil suffered. An industry whose job ramp-up was so meteoric that "if you can spell 'shale,' you can get a job"[84] had laid off those new hires and many more. Nationwide job loss accompanied falling crude oil prices as production and exploration companies cut expenditures and future projects, laid off workers, reduced output. In Alaska alone, the oil and gas industry took a 5.7% loss in jobs in 2015.[85] Certainly mass layoffs can occur in other industries (like banking during the 2008 crash and subsequent recession), but white collar skills can sometimes be shifted more easily to other industries than blue collar skills.

Additionally, it's worth discussing here the differences today between blue collar workers in manufacturing and factories as compared with blue collar workers in other fields such as construction, transportation, energy, etc. Factory work doesn't provide as good a wage rate as it used to: in 2015 durable-goods manufacturing workers made $20.79 an hour in March; private-sector workers overall made $20.89. In other words, "factory workers don't make more than other workers any more....overall, the great factory-worker wage premium has disappeared. Workers in motor-vehicle and motor-vehicle-parts manufacturing, for example, made 50 percent more than private-sector workers in general in the early 1990s. Now the autoworker premium is down to 2 percent."[86] After the recession of 2008 came to an end, manufacturing began to grow, but "the new production jobs created are less likely to be union and more likely to pay low wages. Utilization rates by families of workers employed in manufacturing production occupations through temporary staffing services is even higher, at 50 percent, close to the rate for fast-food workers."[87] The manufacturing sector has become a less desirable place for blue collar workers, being replaced by more lucrative types of blue collar work as discussed in Chapter 6. The reason for this shift may be due in part to outsourcing of work to other countries or to the fact that many manufacturing plants use so much automated technology that the need for trained, skilled workers has decreased.

Temporary Workers

A trend in blue collar employment has been the rise in temporary work. Blue collar construction work is inherently temporary in nature as workers build, demolish, renovate, or remediate themselves out of a job. However, union representation helps keep consistency and stability more alive in those fields. In areas where unions are not as strong and thus are not able to help workers as much, the instability of temporary work can erode some of the benefits of being a blue collar worker. The results of temporary work can be negative including a reduced likelihood of regaining former earnings in a new job and the fact that for that period, no wages are earned.

As a financial planner, the term "temporary work" makes me worry. It's hard enough for people with full-time income they can depend on to manage cash flow well and save for retirement; those who can't count on a regular paycheck have it even harder. If you are a blue collar worker in a temporary employment situation, you need to plan even better than the average person.

A Tough Life

Blue collar work, especially in the construction industry, can be physically harder and more dangerous than office work. Statistics[88] on construction deaths in 2013 show that 20% of workplaces fatalities occurred in the construction industry, primarily from:

- Falls – 302 of 828 total deaths in construction (36.5%)
- Being struck by an object – 84 (10.1%)
- Electrocutions – 71 (8.6%)
- Caught in/between – 21 (2.5%)

Workplace violence[89] is also a bigger problem in blue collar environments. According to OSHA, the percentage of American companies experiencing effects from workplace violence runs about 39%. In some blue collar fields, the percentage is much higher: in the utilities sector it was 69% in 2005 (most recent data available); in the construction sector, 93.1% of companies reported at least one incidence of workplace violence.

Shorter Careers

Although some blue collar workers are blessed with genetics and life habits that allow them to work well past customary retirement ages, most blue collar workers need to retire earlier than most white collar workers. The physical demands of climbing 22-foot scaffolding, tying rebar, setting transmission lines, and other strenuous work are too demanding for a 70-year-old employee to safely and effectively complete the work. At some point, a worker needs to retire. Many retired blue collar workers find second lucrative careers that are less demanding and are able to continue to earn wages. Skills developed over many years can be used to teach, estimate, mentor, substitute, and guide. Even if a second career is possible, the physical demands of your primary career should be considered.

Society's Norms

For some reason, "blue collar" has gotten a bad rap in some circles. Instead of being proud of citizens who build a waste tank, transport crucial supplies, move people around cities, or ensure the electricity and gas keep the world moving, the media and the entertainment world sometimes portray blue collar workers as uneducated, gullible, and dumb. Although you can probably find a few folks whose co-workers view them as such at every place of employment at any level anywhere in the world, blue collar workers certainly don't fit that stereotypical mold.

Despite the growing options for blue collar work, the myth persists that college is the only way to go to be successful. Take a look at the next few sections and consider the potential value of a blue collar career. Matthew B. Crawford writes that "any high school principal who doesn't claim as his or her goal '100% university attendance' is likely to be accused of harboring 'low expectations' and run out of town by indignant parents. That indignation is hard to stand against, as it carries all the moral weight of egalitarianism (every child can be a scholar). Yet it is also snobbish, insofar as it regards the trades as a 'low expectation.' The best sort of democratic education would be neither snobbish nor egalitarian. Rather, it would take its bearings from whatever is best."[90] Crawford's point rings especially true in the case of a high school student who has no interest in attending college but finds him- or herself there because college attendance is an customary practice in the U.S. in this era.

Tom Owens of the North American Building Trades Unions (NABTU) points out that among today's policymakers who contemplate their blue collar constituents "you can almost hear them wondering, privately, where the wrong turn happened. It's almost as if they are asking themselves how any smart, capable person could end up in such an ignoble career. They don't seem to realize, as is the case with the men and women who comprise NABTU, that a tremendous amount of highly technical work – both in the classroom and on the job – is required for them to become certified in their given profession."[91]

Employment journalist Jason Lange sums up the situation in February 2015 as this: "America has added more than a million jobs in the space of three months but wages, especially for blue collar workers, are showing few signs of gains….Eventually it will become harder to find forklift operators, machinists and welders."[92] In some ways, choosing a career as a blue collar worker is a bit of a gamble because the U.S. hasn't reached a crisis point in needed – and therefore financially rewarding – types of blue collar work. However, many white collar jobs are not yielding livable wages, so the decision to choose a blue collar career, even in the case where wages are not at their highest, can be a good one for young people who aren't interested in college. America's future will require trained blue collar employees, and we will pay them well for their skills and abilities.

PAYING FOR BLUE COLLAR TRAINING

What kind of training is required for getting a good blue collar job, and where can you get trained? Today's blue collar jobs aren't without competition nor are they necessarily an "easy" hire. Some blue collar professions only require a high school degree, but many require extensive training, apprenticeships, and years of hard work before you earn the higher salaries that experts command. And the high-tech demands of today's manufacturing and hands-on world will create a "new line of robotics and software that will spawn derivative industries that will … evolve into a more educated, more highly skilled workforce. In this respect, the American laborer may be on track."[93] Appendix 4 lists blue collar jobs and the kind of training or apprenticeships they require.

Blue collar expert Joe Lamacchia in his book, *Blue Collar and Proud of It*, provides an appendix of schools that offer training for many types of blue collar careers (see Appendix 3 of this book for information. In this section, I refer to training for blue collar jobs as "tech school training." You can also go online or call the admissions office of any technical college to get more information about what kinds of careers are out there that you might be interested in and good at. Some blue collar careers may require that you attend (and pay for) some months or years of training: "In two years, a student can earn an associate degree for in-demand professions such as lab technician, computer technician, radiation therapist, and paralegal. Because a postsecondary college focuses on a rigorous and relevant curriculum that clearly prepares a student with job-specific skills, students walk away career-ready, along with an academic degree or professional certification."[94]

I spoke with Dr. Susan Winsor, long-time president of our local technical college, Aiken Technical College in Aiken, SC. She points out that "the nature and demands of the current and upcoming job market are not well-understood. At one time, companies had the ability and finances to run their own comprehensive in-house training programs, but very few can afford to do that today. Therefore, companies want to hire employees who are trained, highly skilled, and ready to work. Aiken Technical College creates those employees…. There is a shortage of blue-collar workers and very robust job opportunities out there."[95]

See Appendix 4 for information on tech school training. The information in this section on college grants and loans applies to 2-year technical colleges and many other types of tech school for blue collar careers. Check with the admissions and financial aid departments of the school you'd like to attend to find out what kind of financial aid you or your child are eligible for.

For a blue collar job in the construction trades, you can sign up with the union of the trade you are interested in pursuing and become an apprentice. The union will provide in-class training and on-the-job training as you work your way through an apprenticeship to become a journeyman worker at the full union rate. Although this process can take 3-4 years, during which time you are paid less per hour than the full journeyman rate, after you complete the program, you can count on earning that rate (with yearly cost of living raises, benefits, and overtime pay) for the rest of your career. And you didn't have to take out a 4-year college loan to get there. See Appendix 5 for information on unions.

According to Anthony Carnevale of the Georgetown University Center on Education and the Workforce, who points out that just for electricians there are 600,000 jobs open in the U.S. today, "The baby-boom workers are retiring and leaving lots of openings for millennials…a big opportunity for that millennial generation born between 1980 and 2000. With so many boomers retiring from the trades, the U.S. is going to need a lot more pipe-fitters, nuclear power plant operators, carpenters, welders, utility workers – the list is long. But the problem is not enough young people are getting that kind of training."[96]

How can you pay for training that you or your children need? If the career you choose requires on-the-job training, you'll be paid while you learn. If you need to attend a school, the section below on paying for college also applies to financial aid for 2-year technical colleges and other training required for a blue collar job. The cool thing about blue collar education is that it costs less and takes less time than a 4-year college degree.

PAYING FOR COLLEGE AND TECH TRAINING

What if your children – or you – want to go to college? Then you should go! The discussions in this book about the value of a blue collar job don't mean that college should be off the table for any of my readers. Advice on how to apply for college and pay for it varies depending on whether we're talking about a high-school student headed there right after graduation or an adult who wants to go back to school. In this section, I'll discuss the basics of college and tech school funding for all types of students. Plenty of books and online sources can provide lots more information, and, in the case of your high school child, the school guidance department in conjunction with the college or tech school he or she plans to attend will guide you every step of the way.

College tuition is expensive – in 2016, private colleges like Vassar and Harvey Mudd cost more than $60,000 per year for tuition, room, and board. Even state schools are expensive, especially when you realize that college expenses entail much more than just the cost of tuition. You also need to pay for housing, food, fees, books, and parking. For example, in 2016, our state school, the University of South Carolina, charges $11,854 for tuition, $7,200 for housing, $3,650 for meals, $200 for the technology fee, and approximately $1,080 for books for a total of $23,984 per year. Whether you go to a local community college or to Stanford, this kind of educational opportunity is expensive. Let's discuss the ways to pay for a college education:

- Personal Savings – regular and tax-advantaged
- Federal, state, college, and private grants and scholarships – need-based
- State, college and private grants and scholarships – merit-based
- Federal, state, college, and private loans

Keep in mind that money from *loans* needs to be re-paid; money provided by *grants* and *scholarships* does not.

Personal College Savings

Most parents of new babies want to start saving right away for their children's college education. The desire to save usually increases as the children get closer to graduation from high school. Unless your family's financial circumstances are very dire, you and/or your child will likely need to pay for some part of college tuition and expenses. What are the best ways to save for college and tech training? You can prepare in advance by saving money for your or your child's college tuition. You can save money in a bank, savings account, money market account, or brokerage account, but you might also want to take advantage of two types of college savings plans that give you tax breaks. Educational Savings Accounts (also referred to as ESAs, Coverdell accounts, or educational IRAs) and College 529 Plans (also called a Qualified Tuition Plan or QTP) are two tax-advantaged ways to save for your child's college education.

A Coverdell ESA is a trust or custodial account set up to pay the qualified educational expenses of a beneficiary. Unlike an IRA or 401(k), the money you contribute is "after-tax" money (money that you have already paid taxes on). When you take the money out, then you don't pay any more taxes on the money that was contributed. If you use the money to pay for educational expenses, they you don't need to pay any tax on the money earned in that account over the years. Should you take the money out and not use it for educational expenses, you would owe a 10% penalty and would have to pay tax on the amount of money earned over the years it was held in the account. You can contribute up to $2,000 per year to a Coverdell account for your child or another child up until the child's 18th birthday. However, your modified adjusted gross income (MAGI) must be less than $110,000 (less than $220,000 if filing a joint return) to participate.[97] All Coverdell money must distributed by the time the designated beneficiary reaches age 30, except in the case of a special needs beneficiary.

A qualified tuition program (QTP) or College 529 Plan is a program set up to allow you to contribute to an account established for paying or to pre-pay a student's qualified education expenses at college or tech school. QTPs can be established and maintained by states and eligible educational institutions. The beneficiary of the account is the student for whom the QTP is intended to provide benefits. The designated beneficiary can be changed after participation in the QTP begins.[98] Total 529 plan contribution limits are set by the states and can be as high as

$380,000. To avoid gift tax consequences, Federal law allows single taxpayers to contribute up to $14,000 in one year or make a lump-sum contribution of $70,000 to cover five years (see information on gift tax in Chapter 5). Married couples may contribute as much as $28,000 per year or $140,000 as a lump sum to a QTP.[99] There are no AGI limits that prevent you from being able to contribute to QTPs as is the case in Coverdell accounts. Another great thing about QTP money is that it can be used for tech school or other vocational schools – not just 4-year colleges – and it can be used for part-time education.[100] There are no age limits with a 529 Plan – either for contributing to it or for using the money. So at age 45 you could set up a 529 plan for yourself to use to go back to college after you retire at age 65 from your current job. When you take the money out, you have to use it to pay for eligible college expenses to avoid taxes and penalties.[101] If you withdraw money from a 529 plan and do not use it on an eligible college expense, you generally will be subject to income tax and an additional 10% Federal tax penalty on earnings. Don't worry – you never "lose" the money you contribute even if the beneficiary doesn't go to school. You always get your contributions back minus the penalty and tax on the earnings. Many states offer residents a break on state income tax or other benefits for investing in a 529 plan.[102]

Grants and Scholarships That Provide Financial Aid for College and Tech School – Need-Based

College aid money is available to students of all ages with levels of financial net worth and yearly income under amounts set by the government. Aid based on your financial situation is called "need-based," and it is determined by completing an online form called the Free Application for Federal Student Aid (FAFSA). Federal Student Aid, a part of the U.S. Department of Education, is the largest provider of student financial aid in the nation.[103] The Federal Student Aid department develops and processes the 22 million FAFSA applications submitted by college candidates each year. They also manage the Federal student loan program.[104]

Let's go over what the FAFSA is and why it's important.[105] Almost all colleges base aid on a document called the FAFSA.[106] They assign and distribute more than $150 billion in Federal grants, loans, and work-study funds to more than 13 million students paying for college or tech school. That's a lot of financial help, and in many cases, you or your child will be eligible for funding or loans determined by completing the FAFSA. You can learn more about the FAFSA and the funding it provides at fafsa.ed.gov.

You can get two types of grants based on financial need from Federal student aid. Keep in mind that a *grant* is a type of financial aid that doesn't have to be paid back in contrast to a loan that must be repaid with interest or a work-study program that offers you a job to earn money to help you pay for school.[107] Need-based grants from the Federal government for education are:

- Federal Pell Grants
- Federal Supplemental Educational Opportunity Grants (FSEOG)

Pell Grants are awarded to undergraduate students in 4-year or 2-year college who have demonstrated financial need. For the 2015-2016 school year, the maximum award is $5,730; next year in 2016-17, the maximum award is $5,815. Depending on your financial need as determined by the FAFSA application and the cost of attendance at the school you plan to go to, you may qualify for no Pell Grant money, some of the award, or the maximum amount for that year. It's always worth completing the FAFSA to see if you are eligible for this grant; even if your income and assets are far above the amount awarded for Pell Grants, other merit-based scholarships may require FAFSA data and most colleges require that students complete the form. In 2016, most Pell Grants are awarded to students whose families make less than $30,000 annually, although families making as much as $60,000 annually may qualify for Pell Grant funds based on number of dependents in the family, how many family members are in college, and how expensive their colleges are.

Federal Supplemental Educational Opportunity Grants (FSEOG), discussed extensively below, are awarded by the college rather than the Federal government to Pell-Grant-qualifying undergraduate students who have exceptional financial need. This grant's maximum value is $4,000 in 2016.

What is the typical financial situation of students who get these grants? Money is awarded based on the family and/or the student's financial situation. Your eligibility depends on your Expected Family Contribution (EFC), your year in school, your enrollment status, and the cost of attendance at the school you will be attending. The financial aid office at your college or tech school will determine how much financial aid you are eligible to receive.[108]

Your EFC is an index number that college financial aid staff uses to determine how much financial aid you would receive if you were to attend their school. The information you report on your FAFSA is used to calculate your EFC. The EFC is calculated according to a formula established by law. Your family's income, assets, and benefits (such as unemployment or Social Security) all could be considered in the formula. Also considered are your family size and the number of family members who will attend college or career school during the year. The EFC formula guide shows exactly how an EFC is calculated. Your EFC is not the amount of money your family will have to pay for college, nor is it the amount of Federal student aid you will receive. It is a number used by your school to calculate how much financial aid you are eligible to receive at that school.[109] The calculation for EFC is complicated. The FAFSA admin team calculates the amount based on the information entered in the application each year. The following steps are complicated but are provided here so you can see the process; the school does all the calculations.

- The financial aid staff starts by deciding on your cost of attendance (COA) at that school.
- They then consider your EFC.
- They subtract your EFC from your COA to determine the amount of your financial need and therefore how much need-based aid you can get.
- To determine how much non-need-based aid you can get, the school takes your COA and subtracts any financial aid you've already been awarded.

Even if you were to receive the full amount of these grants, you would receive just $9,730 in 2016, which is still short of the cost of a year of many colleges. If your financial situation is such that you would qualify for other non-Federal, non-state need-based funds, you'll want to explore those options. Lots of books and websites provide lists of places to apply for need-based grants and scholarships other than governmental funds (see Appendix 6) When you apply for need-based grants, most will use your FAFSA data, and some will request additional financial information like tax returns, SNAP benefit documentation, and statements of net worth. In completing scholarship applications, be sure to:

- Read all instructions
- Apply early and pay attention to due dates
- Send all documents required
- Complete any additional necessary forms
- Keep records of scholarships applied for, due dates, essays written, and information provided
- Follow up on applications

Financial Aid from your State

Your *state* may also offer financial aid. Each state is different in what it might offer for need-based and merit-based aid. In South Carolina, the state provides generous merit-based scholarships funded by a lottery to high school residents who attend college in SC. The Life scholarship of $5,000 and the Palmetto Fellow scholarship of $6,700 per year for 4 years in 2016 are awarded to high school residents who meet the academic criteria.

The FAFSA is discussed above, but in addition to completing your FAFSA,[110] you want to be sure to complete the follow-on steps to the FAFSA that help you and your child nail down more college financial aid from your *state*. How can you maximize the amount of state need-based aid your student can get from the college he or she plans to attend? Let's take a look at the steps involved and the deadlines you want to meet.

In addition to Pell Grant money, each state also gets some funding from the Federal government to administer to students with financial need. This grant is called the Federal Supplemental Educational Opportunity Grant (FSEOG),[111] and as with other grants, they don't need to be paid back. The FSEOG may be supplemented by other state need-based grants whose titles vary from state to state. This grant money is awarded to the student in addition to Federal aid. Unlike Federally administered FAFSA funds, FSEOG funds are awarded by the college your student attends and tend to run out early in the award year. Therefore, if you fall into a category where your EFC is low because your Adjusted Gross Income (AGI) is low or because you have many dependents and more than one student in college, you want to make sure you quickly complete all the requirements needed in addition to the FAFSA to put your student at the head of the line for receiving these state need-based funds.

Each college is somewhat different in the steps they require before your student is able to receive an FSEOG need-based award; however, the following tips apply to every school.

- Make sure your child has formally enrolled at the college and has officially let the college know that he or she is going to attend there.
- Call the college's financial aid department and get to know the counselors there; write down their names and contact info for future reference in case you need it.
- Have your student set up and check his or her college-issued email account regularly because some colleges communicate through that account as soon as the student is enrolled; not accessing and checking that account can mean that you miss key communications.
- Have your child enroll in the electronic system the college uses to post financial aid status; access the site regularly to see what documents are still missing.
- Even though you and your student complete the FAFSA early, check to make sure the college has it on file. Clear up any disconnects or problems as quickly as possible.
- Try to do your taxes early in the tax season if possible. W-2s come out by January 31, but if you have investments, you may not have all the documents you need to file until March. In that case, the college will probably allow you to send W-2s for the current year to verify your income.

- If you file your taxes later in the year via a tax extension request, the school will have a form to complete to indicate that plan and to submit your complete IRS Form 4868, Request for Extension to File. The school will use your current year W-2s to determine eligibility.
- Once you've completed your current year tax return, the FAFSA has a system called the Data Retrieval Tool (DRT) that lets you transmit an official version of your tax return to the college so that they can see if your student is eligible for the FSEOG or another state need-based grant. Complete this action as soon as it is turned on in your and your child's FAFSA online accounts.
- Use scanning and faxing rather than regular mail to speed up response times. If the college website says it mails forms, call them to ask about emailing and faxing. It's worth the cost even if you have to pay at Staples to scan or fax documents because timing is so important.
- Schools have an early cut-off date for state-based funds because they are so limited and need is so great. The "priority date" is often not readily available on the school's website, so call the financial aid office to find it out. Then beat the date by making sure that all your required information is submitted and has been processed by the school.

Even if you have submitted most of the documents required, until you have them all, your student is not in the state need-based grant line. He or she is *near* the line, but just like at Disney World, you are not going on the ride if you aren't actually *in* line. If the priority award date for these state funds passes before your student is standing in the queue, he or she will probably not receive any assistance from this source. In many states, once this state money has been awarded, it is gone for that school year. You can get back in line next year, but this year's window closes after the deadline.

Even if you think it is unlikely you will qualify for Federal or state need-based funds, be sure to complete college financial aid action items as quickly as possible to ensure that your student ends up with the greatest amount of financial aid he or she qualifies for.

Grants and Scholarships That Provide Financial Aid for College – Merit-Based

Need-based funds to help pay for college may be available to you or to your children. However, your family may have too high an income or net worth to be eligible for need-based grants. Merit-based grants, which are based on test grades, class rank, athletic skills, club membership, extracurricular activities, and other life experiences, can also be a source of college money. A high-school kid's financial future can depend a lot on choices he or she makes in high school. Few decisions are irreparable, but high school achievements and activities often go a long way to determining your adult life-style and financial safety. Your child's high school experience, including grades, SAT/ACT scores, sports, and extracurricular activities can lead to money for college. It's worth it to encourage and support your child in taking part in activities he or she enjoys. Our daughter played volleyball in high school. She wasn't good enough to be recruited for an athletic scholarship, but she played as a walk-on at the University of South Carolina. Her status as an athlete allowed her to get lots of free clothes and bags, register early for the best teachers and classes, connect with athletes and coaches, and enjoy trips with the team. Additionally, it's usually a better payoff for your child to put time into getting good grades and high test stores rather than work at an $8 an hour waitressing job.

Your own memberships and connections can also lead to college money – the company you work for, organizations you are a part of, and places you volunteer may offer scholarships to students headed to college. Ask and do research to find out what scholarships are out there, then take the time to apply. Some of the applications can be a time-consuming hassle, but you can think about the effort in terms of the return. If you spend 3 hours completing a scholarship application that nets you $3,000 of tax-free college money, that works out to about to $1,000 per hour! Good places to find out about scholarship opportunities include the reference librarian at your local public or university library and knowledgeable salespeople at bookstores. The high school guidance department will probably let you know about scholarship opportunities for your student to apply for. Appendix 6 provides information on college scholarships. When you apply for merit-based grants, most will use your FAFSA data and will require essays about why you should receive the scholarship. In completing scholarship applications, be sure to:

- Read all instructions
- Apply early and pay attention to due dates
- Send all documents required
- Complete any additional necessary forms
- Keep records of scholarships applied for, due dates, essays written, and information provided
- Follow up on applications

Two more educational grants from the Federal government are based on career activities, past or future. **Iraq and Afghanistan Service Grants** of up to $5,311.71 are given to students with a parent who was a member of the U.S. armed forces and died as a result of performing military service in Iraq or Afghanistan after the events of 9/11. **Teacher Education Assistance for College and Higher Education (TEACH) Grants** are given regardless of need to students who are going to school to become elementary or secondary teachers. This $4,000-per-year grant is more like a work-study arrangement; if you receive this funding, after graduation you have to teach full-time for at least 4 years in a high-need field in a school or educational service agency that serves low-income students. If you fall short of the requirements, your grant is converted to a Direct Unsubsidized Loan you have to repay.

College Loans That Provide Financial Aid for College

If you've exhausted all possibilities for need- and merit-based grants and you don't have enough savings or current income to cover college or tech school costs, you may need to borrow money to attend college or to pay for other training. Subsidized and unsubsidized student loans from the government or private loans may provide part of that funding. In general, schools expect parents (or the students themselves for returning adult students) to contribute a maximum of 5.64 percent of assets. Dependent students are expected to contribute up to 35 percent of their assets and 50 percent of their income.

We've read and heard about the crippling student loan debt so many in the millennial generation are burdened with. The difficulties these young people face shouldn't be minimized, but it's important to realize that a reasonable amount of student loan debt is not to be feared. It's unrealistic for most of us to be able to accumulate in the 18 subsequent years of our newborn's life the tens of thousands of dollars needed to pay for a college education. What's a reasonable amount of money to borrow? Compare these examples. If you are taking a $5,000-a-year loan to earn a degree as an engineer in a state university in a state where you reside, it makes sense that with your future $70,000-a-year engineering job, you'll be able to pay that $20,000 loan back with relative ease. However, if you decide to go to a private, out-of-state college for a photography degree and borrow $20,000 a year to cover the costs, you will probably be hard pressed to pay back $80,000 of student loan debt on the freelance art job making $18,000 per year that you are likely to end up with. When you choose a college and a major, you want to be realistic about the salary you are likely to earn when you graduate so that you can take out manageable student loans that you can afford to pay back without dramatically compromising your lifestyle.

These are the types of college loans students may qualify for:

- Federal Stafford ("Direct") loan
- Perkins loan
- Federal PLUS loan
- Private college loan
- Home-equity loan
- Cash-value life insurance
- Some retirement accounts

The U.S. Department of Education offers Federal student loans[112]:

- Stafford (or "Direct") Subsidized Loans are loans made to eligible undergraduate students who demonstrate financial need. In this type of loan, the government pays the interest while the student is in school, during grace periods, and during any deferment periods; the borrower pays interest accrued after graduation. The fact that the government pays the interest for you during your four years of college is a really good deal; the interest is not "deferred" until you graduate but rather is paid for you. Once you graduate, you begin to repay the interest and the principal.

- Stafford (or "Direct") Unsubsidized Loans are loans made to eligible undergraduate, graduate, and professional students, but in this case, the student does not have to demonstrate financial need to be eligible for the loan. Interest in unsubsidized loans is paid by the borrower, not the government.

- The Federal Perkins Loan Program is a school-based loan program for undergraduates and graduate students with exceptional financial need. Undergrad students can borrow up to $5,500 per year in Perkins Loans depending on financial need, the amount of other aid received, and the availability of funds at the college or career school.

- Direct PLUS Loans are loans made to graduate or professional students and parents of dependent undergraduate students to help pay for education expenses not covered by other financial aid. Interest is charged during all periods. First-year undergraduates are eligible for loans up to $5,500. Amounts increase for subsequent years of study, with higher amounts for graduate students. The interest rates may vary based on when the loan is borrowed.[113]

The interest rate on Federal student loans is almost always lower than that on private loans – and much lower than that on a credit card. You don't need a credit check or a cosigner to get most Federal student loans. You don't have to begin repaying your Federal student loans until after you leave college or drop below half-time attendance. Federal student loans offer flexible repayment plans and options to postpone your loan payments if you're having trouble making payments. If you work in certain jobs, you may be eligible to have a portion of your Federal student loans forgiven if you meet certain conditions. Loan rates in 2016 range from 4.26% (fixed rate for a Direct Federal Stafford Loan) to 6.84% for a Parent PLUS loan. Private college loan rates may be higher.

In general, private loans are not subsidized or need-based. They also often require a cosigner – someone who promises to repay the money if the student fails to do so. The interest rates of private loans vary:

- Banks tend to have the highest interest rates.
- Some private organizations offer lower interest rates.
- Some colleges offer loans with relatively low interest rates.

Although the following loan choices tend to be less desirable than the other options discussed above, you can also consider a home-equity loan, retirement account, or a cash-value life insurance policy as vehicles for college tuition. Financial planners generally advise against using your home, your retirement account, or your insurance to pay for your child's or your own college tuition, but these accounts are sources of money if you have no other choice. A benefit of these accounts is that the interest rate to borrow from them will likely be less than the rate for a private loan. In the case of a home-equity loan, where you borrow with your home as collateral, you take the risk of losing your home if for some reason you are unable to pay the loan back. If you borrow from your 401(k) retirement account and can't pay the money back in the period specified or if your job comes to an end and you are required to pay it back immediately, you could be in a jam. Your cash value life insurance policy may allow you to withdraw a certain amount of the paid premiums without paying taxes or a penalty or take out a loan from the insurance company using the cash value of the policy as collateral, but fees and other charges may reduce the value and usefulness of this method.

Financial Aid Considerations for Adults Going to College
The grant, scholarship, and loans discussed above apply to high school students and returning adult students. If you are thinking about going back to college or taking training for a skilled job, you may also be eligible for a Pell Grant or other need-based grants. The financial aid programs discussed above apply to all students regardless of age. When a high-school student applies for aid, the FAFSA takes into account the earnings of the student and his or her family. Young students are considered "dependents," so the entire family's financial situation is taken into account. And you

can't just declare yourself "independent" from your family – the FAFSA has very specific rules about who is and is not a dependent. Based on 2016 guidelines, most high school students fall into the "dependent" category unless they are married, supporting their own children, foster children, homeless, ex-military, older than age 23, or a few other exceptions.[114] As an adult returning to school, aid determinations are based on your own income and assets.

If you are out of high school and working on your own, you will be eligible for grant money based on your own financial situation, not your parents, even if you are still living with them. For example, back in the late 1970s, I went to the U.S. Naval Academy. I was in one of the first classes that accepted women, and after two years there, I realized that I was not a good fit. I resigned and went back home to live with my parents. Even though I was 19 years old and back at the house with mom and dad, I was considered "independent" for financial aid purposes and I received a Pell Grant to finish out my degree at the College of William and Mary. If you have a job and are thinking of going back to school full-time or part-time, you may qualify for grant money. It's worth taking the time to fill out and submit a FAFSA.

An additional thought for potential students who would like to go back to school is to check with your current employer about tuition assistance. One of the fringe benefits an employer can offer tax-free to its employees is up to $5,250 (in 2016) of money annually for tuition and expenses. It's a little known benefit that is often not advertised well. A company I worked for offered that benefit, and through that program I earned an MBA. I found a program that offered classes nights and weekends; it took 5 years, but I ended up with an advanced degree and no cost to me. I can still remember sitting in a dark, smoky, beer-soaked old ski lodge studying for a statistics exam while my husband and kids were out on the slopes! You can usually tap in to company tuition assistance for all kinds of classes and training – it doesn't have to be for a 4-year degree. And if you are thinking of changing careers, you could work full-time at your current job and go to school nights and weekends on their dime; then you apply for jobs in your new field after having earned your full salary and had your school paid for. Be sure to check your employer's policy on tuition reimbursement since some employers

116

require that you stay at your current job for some period of time after tuition reimbursement or else have to pay the money back.

If the program or major you want to take makes it impossible to keep your current job full time, ask if you can work for them part time or on a consulting basis so that you can keep bringing in some cash while going to school. Up to $5,250 in these benefits can be tax-free each year, according to the IRS – as long as it's put toward tuition, books, and supplies. The Society for Human Resource Management's 2015 Employee Benefits report found 56% of the employers surveyed helped employees pay for undergraduate studies and 52% helped them pay for graduate studies. The average maximum benefit was $4,591. If your company offers tuition reimbursement, ask your human resources representative about the rules and requirements. For example, you may have to stay at the company for a certain amount of time after you graduate or else be required to pay the tuition assistance back.

Ways to Minimize College Costs

Whether you are a high school student or a working adult going back to college, consider these ideas for reducing the cost of going to college. First, use the information above to maximize your college financial aid. Another idea is to start your college experience at a smaller, local college near your home. For example, the difference in the cost of tuition and fees between the main university in our state, the University of South Carolina (USC), and a branch of that college, the University of South Carolina – Aiken (USCA), is $5894 per year. In 2016, USC charges $11,854 for tuition, $7,200 for housing, $3,650 for meals, $200 for the technology fee, and approximately $1,080 for books for a total of $23,984; USCA charges $9,588 for tuition, $4,470 for housing, $2,550 for meals, $132 for the technology fee, and approximately $1,080 for books for a total of $18,090. For an Aiken resident, a great way to save money and still get a degree from a big university (with a football team!) might be to attend USCA for two years while living at home to save even more and transfer to USC for your last two years. Most states have similar financial differentials between their main colleges and local branches. A third path that could save money is to consider enlisting in the military where you'll gain experience and skills and then be able to take advantage of the GI Bill for financial assistance when you get out and go back to school. You could also join the military Reserve Officers' Training Corp (ROTC) at the college you attend for financial help. Another possibility is living at home and getting your degree online. You miss out on the college "experience" this way, but it can be a potentially smart move. Online degrees used to be regarded with suspicion in the work world, but they are becoming more and more acceptable. Another idea is to investigate colleges not near your home that are known for low tuition costs. These universities are not in the most exciting locations – two are in North Dakota! – but if you're committed to getting a college degree and finances are tight, it might be an option. Finally, make sure you get all the tax breaks you are eligible for as a result of paying college tuition and fees. You may be able to take tax deduction for college costs or one of the education tax credits, the American Opportunity Tax Credit or the Lifetime Learning Credit.[115]

Conclusion

Education and training can open the door to a great career. It's important to weigh the cost of school against the benefit you would likely get from being trained in a particular job. Most of us have many different interests and would excel in several career paths. Make sure you choose a major or career field that you think you will be good at and like AND that pays well if possible.

CHAPTER 5
RETIREMENT

Retirement planning is an important part of good financial health. Numerous books, articles, and websites out there can give specific advice and recommend reasonable actions for you to take toward ensuring you have enough money after you retire. This book offers general suggestions about planning for retirement with a concentration on retiring from a blue collar career. As you prepare for retirement, you need to take into account traditional ideas for sound financial planning as well as several factors unique to blue collar work including the physical demands of the work, the potential for layoff periods, and the chance that you may have changed companies many times over your career.

GENERAL ADVICE FOR RETIREMENT PLANNING

As a financial planner, I am often called on to help with retirement planning. At some point, when a person no longer wishes to work or is unable to work, he or she needs to have enough money to pay living expenses. Most retired workers have Social Security retirement benefits. However, even if you earn the absolute highest monthly amount possible because you earned the maximum in lifetime wages, the most you can possibly receive monthly from Social Security in 2016 is $2,639. Most people will receive much less. At the max amount of $2,639 per month (for one person), your individual yearly income would be about $30,000. According the Social Security Administration, the average monthly benefit for retirees in 2016 was $1,335 per month or $16,020 per year.[116] That amount is not very far above the 2016 Federal Poverty Line amount for one person of $11,880.[117] For retirees with no savings and no pension, it would be tough to meet basic living expenses on

119

Social Security income alone. Since fewer and fewer people are retiring with pension money, and the average person in his or her 80's or 90's would be hard pressed to find a job, there is little prospect for bringing in extra cash. That's why financial planners work to encourage people to save for retirement during their working years even if it seems difficult or impossible to do so. Planning is just as important for people in blue collar jobs. What are the key components of a good retirement plan?

- Monthly retirement income and expenses (from Social Security, pension, distributions from retirement savings, dividends, or part-time work)
- Retirement savings (from 401(k)s, IRAs, or general savings and investments)
- Housing (including possible nursing home care)
- Health insurance (Medicare after age 65)
- Legacy planning (leaving money to children or charities)

Retirement Income and Expenses
How will you support yourself when you no longer receive a paycheck? Where will the money come from each month to pay for a place to live, food to eat, medicine and medical care, and other basic living expenses? If you were to visit a financial planner, one of the key tasks you'd complete with your planner is an analysis of how much you currently have saved for retirement, how much you think you will need during retirement, and how much you should to save between now and retirement to get there. This exercise is a pleasant and reassuring one for wealthy people who earn high salaries and have the promise of pension plan money for the rest of their lives. It's less so for the 90+% of the rest of the country whose salaries or wages are often not sufficient to support a comfortable lifestyle for themselves and their families today, much less save for retirement in a meaningful way to ensure sufficient retirement income to meet expenses in old age.

In the past, you might have counted on pension money to support you during your retirement years. My Nana lived to age 100 and was sent $226 per month for 40 years from her career in the meat department of Clemens Supermarket. The amount certainly was small, but it functioned as regular and reliable cash flow each month. Today, pensions are being phased out in the workplace, so few of us will receive regular payments from our former jobs when we retire. In my case, I never worked for a company that offered pensions, and it's even more unlikely that my young adult kids will ever have the chance to earn a pension. In the past, when people only lived into their 60's and companies weren't subject to as many buyouts, it made sense to offer a guaranteed benefit lifetime pension to long-time workers who retired after years with the company. It makes much less business sense today in 2016. As people live well into their 80's and 90's and companies merge and change hands, company pension plans have become rare. The pension plan has been replaced by the company 401(k), which can be a useful retirement savings too, but as I discuss below, it offers fewer guarantees of solid income than pensions did.

So what can you do to make sure enough cash is coming in each month during your retirement years? Let's talk about a few ideas:

- Working part-time
- Maximizing Social Security benefits
- Applying for government or charitable assistance
- Using a reverse mortgage
- Relying on dividends from investments
- Taking money from savings and investment accounts
- Collecting from your pension plan

Working Part Time

How about working part time? Even if you don't want to continue your full time career, you may find that a part time job in the same field or a different one ensures that your mind stays sharp. Working 20 hours a week on a flexible schedule is much more pleasant than having to get up early five days a week and fight daily work traffic. Regardless of your current career, it's very likely that you'll be able to find interesting part time work in your golden years. The changing nature of blue collar work as a contracted business also lends itself to working after retirement, and you can set up shop using internet sources like Angie's List, IWanta, Elance, and many other sites. You may find that your skills as a carpenter, automotive technician, police officer, or truck driver can be parlayed into part time or consulting work that brings in cash but provides a less stressful working life for you.

Maximizing Social Security benefits

You'll probably need to rely on your Social Security benefits for financial stability, so you want them to be as big as they can legally be. Social Security expert Larry Kotlikoff, who wrote *Get What's Yours: The Secrets to Maxing Out Your Social Security*, thinks that life's biggest danger isn't dying but rather "outliving your savings," and the best way to mitigate that danger is "to be patient in taking [Social Security] benefits because they can be bigger – much bigger – if you wait."[118] Although you *can* start your Social Security benefits as early as age 62 (or even age 60 as a widow or widower), the monthly amount will be much smaller than if you are in the financial position to be able to wait. However, waiting is not always the right choice either. Each option should be evaluated, taking into account your own personal circumstances.

Here's an example – Retiree A is 62, with a full retirement age (FRA) of 66. If he starts taking benefits at 62, he gets $1,200 a month. If he waits until age 66, he receives 33% more, or $1,600 a month. He decides to wait until age 70 to take benefits, so his payments increase another 32%, to $2,112 a month for the rest of his life. He ends up living to age 89, and his lifetime benefits are about $38,000, or 13% higher, because he waited until age 70 to collect benefits. Plus, as he gets older, he has the comfort of knowing that $2,112 is coming in each month, which is much better than the $1,200 he would be getting had he started at age 62. Of course, this choice is not without drawbacks. Even though he is paid more money in total by having waited, Retiree A technically could have been investing the $1,200 that came in each month over the 8 years between when he was 62 and 70, which could possibly have earned him more money. On the other hand, take Retiree B, who also decides to delay taking benefits at age 62 and to gamble that he will also live long enough to collect the higher amount. Unfortunately, Retiree B doesn't live until age 89. When he dies 2 years later at age 64, he hasn't collected any money from Social Security. He paid into the Social Security system for his entire 40-year career but dies before he gets a penny of benefits. It can be frustrating when that scenario occurs. Although Retiree B is no longer with us to say "I should have started those benefits at 62," you can bet he'd be complaining if he were alive and able to!

So when is the best time to start taking Social Security benefits? Unfortunately, there's no "one-size-fits-all" answer. If you need the money to pay your monthly expenses, then of course you will start your benefits as soon as you can get them. If you *don't* need the money right away, the decision is harder. Take them too early and you'll kick yourself on your 100th birthday. Take them too late and you lose out on money that is rightfully yours. According to data compiled by the Social Security Administration, a man reaching age 65 today (2016) can expect to live, on average, until age 84.3; a woman turning age 65 today can expect to live, on average, until age 86.6. About one out of every four 65-year-olds today will live past age 90, and one out of 10 will live past age 95.[119] Making this decision is a bit of a gamble. If you have great health and come from a family blessed with longevity, you will probably want to delay benefits if you don't need the money. If your health isn't great and few of your family members lived to a very old age, you may want to start at age 62 to make sure you see at least part of the money due to you from a lifetime of contributing to the Social Security system.

Chapter 1 covers some of the basics of the Social Security system, and you can learn more about your own social security benefits at www.ssa.gov when you set up a "My SSA" account online.

Applying for Government or Charitable Assistance
If your monthly income isn't sufficient to meet your needs in retirement, you may want to consider asking for help from your local government, charities, or churches. If your only source of income is Social Security and you can't work, you may be eligible for assistance like the SNAP program (food stamps), Medicaid, Meals on Wheels, and many other programs for the elderly. The American Association of Retired Persons (AARP) has a great website[120] to research benefits you might qualify for. You can also check with the reference librarian at your local public or college library, your local Council on Aging, the Chamber of Commerce, or the Department of Social Services in your town.

Using a Reverse Mortgage

One way you might be able to generate monthly income if you own your home or if you have substantial equity in it is a reverse mortgage. Reverse mortgages, first offered in the 1960s, were a financial disaster when they become popular in the 1980s, but in 2016, financial planners recommend certain types of reverse mortgages in some situations. Here's how a reverse mortgage works: "after years of paying down your mortgage, you have built up equity (the amount your property is worth today minus the amount you owe on your mortgage and any home equity loan or line of credit) in your home. With a reverse mortgage, you borrow against your equity….The loan balance grows over time. You don't have to pay back the loan while you or an eligible spouse live in the home, but you still have to pay taxes, insurance, and maintain the home. When both you and any eligible spouse have passed away or moved out of the home, the loan must be paid off. Most people need to sell their home to pay off the loan. But, neither you nor your heirs will have to pay back more than your home is worth."[121]

There are three kinds of reverse mortgages: single purpose reverse mortgages which are the least expensive option and are usually used to pay property taxes and home repairs; proprietary reverse mortgages which are private loans that allow you to use the money for any purpose; and Federally-insured reverse mortgages also known as Home Equity Conversion Mortgages (HECMs). An HECM is FHA's reverse mortgage program, which enables you to withdraw some of the equity in your home. To be eligible for an FHA HECM, the FHA requires that you "be a homeowner 62 years of age or older, own your home outright, or have a low mortgage balance that can be paid off at closing with proceeds from the reverse loan, have the financial resources to pay ongoing property charges including taxes and insurance, and live in the home."[122] In a reverse mortgage, you usually don't pay back the money for as long as you live in your home. When you die, sell your home, or move out, you, your spouse, or your estate would repay the loan. Sometimes that means selling the home to repay the loan.[123] It's important to note that your children are not responsible for your debts when you die. If you were to get a reverse mortgage and continue to live in your home beyond the period when all the equity has been used, your children would not be required to pay the reverse mortgage company that money after you die if for some reason your estate was not sufficient to pay off the loan. It's true that their inheritance could be reduced if money from your estate was used to pay off the loan, but they would not be required to come up with extra cash on their own to pay it off after your death. If the value of the home decreased and there wasn't enough equity in the house to re-pay the loan, the mortgage company would take the house as collateral but not make your heirs pay the difference from their own personal funds.

A reverse mortgage might be just the thing you need to make your retirement work financially. Be sure to do research to make sure that you are getting a safe reverse mortgage designed to protect you and your spouse. Keep in mind that all reverse mortgages have fees, and you want to be sure you're not working with a salesperson whose aim is to get you to use the reverse mortgage money to buy their financial products, such as insurance or an annuity.

Relying on Dividends from Investments

One possible income stream in retirement could come from owning stocks that pay dividends. As discussed in Chapter 2, some companies pay "dividends" to their shareholders, which are cash payments for owning the stock. Regular dividend payment dates are set by a company, so you know when you'll receive your dividends. Assuming you continue to own the same number of shares and the company doesn't reduce or eliminate its dividend (which it legally can do at any time), you count on that amount of cash coming in every quarter to cover some of your expenses. Investors sometimes plan stock ownership to ensure a certain level of cash flow. If you were to own shares in companies with dividend payouts in each month of the year, you could have a planned monthly income stream. For example, you've got monthly cash coming in if you own stock in Companies A, B, and C when Company A pays dividends quarterly in January, April, July, and October; Company B pays in February, May, August, and November; and Company C pays in March, June, September, and December. However, this retirement cash flow plan is not foolproof. The problem with this system is that companies are under no obligation to maintain dividend payments to common stockholders. If a company that has traditionally paid a dividend loses value, you face the double whammy of losing your dividend income stream AND owning stock that has declined in value perhaps to an amount that is less than what you paid for it.

Taking Money From Savings and Investment Accounts

If you have money saved for retirement, you'll probably begin to spend that money when you stop working. You can make your own decisions about when and how much to take out of non-retirement accounts. For tax-advantaged retirement accounts like IRAs and 401(k), you have to take distributions on a government-determined schedule.[124] These "Required Minimum Distributions" (RMDs) must start when you turn 70½. The custodian who administers your IRA or 401(k) will probably help make sure you take the correct amounts out, but you want to be aware of the rules so that you don't incur any penalties The reason for these RMDs is because the money in them has not yet been subject to income tax. If you think about it from an IRS tax standpoint, RMDs make sense. When you contributed to your Traditional IRA as a young person, you didn't have to pay any tax on that money then. The money continued to sit there untaxed – and hopefully growing! – during your working years. Traditional IRA money is only taxed when it is withdrawn. So the government wants to make sure it collects the tax due on that money, so it institutes RMDs to make sure you take that money out and pay the tax that is owed. You can take *more* out than specified by the RMD tables, but if you take *less*, you'll pay a 50% excise tax on the amount not distributed. Note that Roth IRAs are not subject to RMDs because the money you've contributed to them is after-tax money.

Collecting From Your Pension Plan

If you are among the lucky Americans who get a pension, you'll be able to count on a life-time income stream to help support you. For most of us, however, pension plans have gone the way of the rotary dial phone. Without a pension, those planning for retirement have to use 401(k) plans, IRAs, and other savings methods to generate money during the retirement years. Unfortunately, the investments in these plans don't guarantee a benefit the way pension plans do. Towers Watson, the global human resources consultant, found that "pension-style plans beat 401(k)-style offerings by nearly 3 percentage points in 2011, the latest study year. Pensions made investment returns of 2.74% while defined contribution plans lost money, banking -0.22%."[125] With a pension plan, you and your spouse will receive monthly payments for life; with a "defined contribution plan" (IRA, 401(k), 403(b), etc.), when the money is gone, you receive no more payments. You can outlive your money and find yourself in difficult financial circumstances.

Another concern with pension funds is if the company or government entity that pays you will continue to have enough money to pay its pension benefits. A government pension insurance company, the Pension Benefit Guarantee Corporation (PBGC), insures private industry pensions, but only up to certain amounts. If a company underfunds its pension and subsequently goes out of business, it may not be able to meet its pension obligations. As pointed out by Michael Fletcher of the *Washington Post*, "the stock market has soared more than 75 percent in the past five years, yet many pension funds, where many middle-class workers should benefit from the market's rise, continue to struggle, jeopardizing benefits for the workers who were counting on them in retirement. At the end of last year, Congress passed legislation allowing certain distressed pension plans to slash retirement benefits, including those already being received by retirees – an unprecedented move altering a principle enshrined in Federal law for four decades that said benefits already earned could not be cut….This change in the social contract is growing more common as employers…increasingly view the mushrooming cost of pensions as unbearable, even as the broader economy recovers."[126] In May of 2016, the court rejected the request to cut benefits, saving for today the pension benefits for those workers, but now the conversation has begun about the possibility of cutting a once-inviolable benefit. In the future, the security of knowing you have pension money coming in may be not a safe assumption even for those with "guaranteed" pensions.

RETIREMENT SAVINGS

You've heard a lot about how Americans today aren't saving enough for retirement. Statistics bear that out: in 2016, about 28% of respondents age 55 and over have *no* retirement savings and 26% report retirement savings with balances of under $50,000, an amount that is insufficient for people nearing retirement age. Only 1 in 4 people age 55 and over had more than $300,000 saved.[127] GenX'ers aren't doing much better: about 30% of that generation has no retirement account and for the 70% who do, in more than half of those accounts the balance is less than $50,000, which is far short of what is needed for a 20 +year retirement.[128] A low rate of savings coupled with increased longevity and reduced likelihood of receiving pension benefits from your work make the prospect of retiring even scarier.

I can think of lots of good reasons why so many Americans aren't able to save for retirement. One reason is that wages for most of us have not risen much over our careers. Housing values in many places in the U.S. have also not increased appreciably. Although inflation has not officially risen substantially, life is more expensive – housing and cars cost more; college tuition has gone up; clothes and food must continually be replaced. Costs that didn't exist when I was little, like cell phone bills, $4 lattes, and video game rentals, ding us and prevent us from saving. TV, the internet, and movies continually seduce us to buy and spend. As a result, many Americans have a small…or empty…retirement account.

How do you figure out how much you need for retirement? A financial planner will run calculations based on your expected life span and the amount of money you expect to spend each year in retirement. Planners generally choose from two traditional methods to determine your retirement financial needs. An income replacement analysis relies on your ballpark estimate of your current income from which a standard percentage of retirement income is established. A retirement income analysis looks at actual cash flow to create a budget for retirement that you then would aim to save for. You can hire a financial planner to help you estimate your retirement needs or use online financial calculators (see Appendix 7) to figure it out for yourself.

Those analyses are helpful and telling, but if you haven't saved anything and aren't saving now, how do you figure out how you will manage in retirement in the real world you live in today? Where do you start and how do you maximize what you do save? Let's talk about the kinds of accounts that Americans in 2016 use to save for retirement.

The rules for retirement plans can be confusing. Differing limits and requirements relating to contributions, withdrawals, income, and taxes can make it difficult to determine the best places for your savings. There are entire courses dedicated to the intricacies of the various plans, but you can learn the basics with just a few key details. The two main types of tax-deferred retirement accounts are the 401(k) and the Individual Retirement Account (IRA). A 401(k) is a retirement savings plan offered to you through your work and managed by your employer. An IRA, on the other hand, is a retirement savings plan that you set up and manage on your own.

There are two primary types of IRAs: Traditional and Roth. The main differences between them lie in *when* you pay tax and *what* you pay tax on. With a Traditional IRA, you get to defer your taxes in the year you make a contribution to your IRA or 401(k). Tax deferral means that you don't owe taxes that year on the money you just contributed (so if you contribute in 2016 your 2016 tax bill is reduced), but you will owe taxes on money you take out of the account later on in retirement. The assumption is that you will be in a lower tax bracket when you withdraw the money in retirement, so you end up paying less in taxes later than if you had paid the tax upfront. With a Roth IRA, you *do* pay taxes on your contributions (so the money you contribute in a given year is **not** tax-deferred), but when you withdraw the money in retirement, you don't have to pay tax again. The interesting thing about a Roth IRA that makes it a good deal as I write this in 2016 is that the money you earn over the years that you are holding the money in your Roth IRA is never taxed – not during the years of holding or when you withdraw it. For an example, say that you contribute $4,000 of after-tax money a year to a Roth IRA for 30 years, making a total contribution of $4,000 times 30 or $120,000. Say that your investments over the 30 years in that Roth IRA made you $10,000. When you take this $10,000 out, you don't have to pay tax on that money. In the IRS tax world, very few tax-free good deals like this exist.

A 401(k) is an employer-sponsored plan that gives employees a choice of investment options. A 401(k) is similar to an IRA in that it lets you pay tax later on money you earn this year. As in an IRA, that benefit reduces your taxes for the given year and saves money that you can invest and grow. A 401(k) is only available to you through a company; you can't start and contribute to one on your own as you can with an IRA. If you work for Federal or state government, you'll contribute to a plan similar to a 401(k) called a 457 plan or 403(b) plan. Some employers match a portion of an employee's 401(k) contributions; if your employer matches, it's important to save enough in that 401(k) to get the match since that's like getting a higher salary.

For all these plans, you need to earn money in that year in order to contribute. For example, if you didn't work and get paid for the work in 2016, you wouldn't be able to contribute any money to an IRA, unless you met special requirements where your spouse earned money that can function as your own earnings.

As a quick refresher: in contrast to regular joint checking/savings/investment accounts, 401(k)s, IRAs and Roth IRAs are individual retirement accounts that are owned only by one person. The money, when withdrawn, can certainly be shared with another person, but only the owner of the retirement account has control over and access to those dollars during his/her lifetime. After death, the money can be left to another person. In divorce, retirement account money is usually split between spouses if the marriage lasted a certain amount of time.

The key component in the success of these plans is to use them – it's important to try and make the commitment to put money in your retirement plan every month and to monitor your investments in the hope of earning the best return possible.

Traditional IRAs, Roth IRAs, and 401(k)s differ in a number of ways including tax treatment, contribution and income limits, and rules for withdrawals when you reach a certain age. The chart below illustrates how tax treatment, income, and contribution rules vary across the most common retirement plan types:

	401(k)	Traditional IRA	Roth IRA
Tax treat-ment	Contributions: **tax-deferred.** Put in money you've **not paid income tax on.** Pay taxes on money you take out, both contributions & investment earnings.	Contributions: **tax-deferred.** Put in money you've **not paid income tax on.** Pay taxes on money you take out, both your contributions & investment earnings.	Contributions: **post-tax.** Put in money you've **already paid tax on.** Taxable income not reduced. Withdrawals during retirement **tax-free.** Benefit of Roth: not paying tax on investment earnings as in traditional IRA.
Contri-bution limits	The most you can contribute to a 401(k) in 2016 is **$18,000.**	The maximum tax-deferred contribution for 2016 is **$5,500.** If you are covered by a retirement plan at work – such as a 401(k) – there may be a limit to how much of your contribution is tax-deferred, depending on your income (see below). If you are not covered by a retirement plan at work, you can contribute the full amount tax-deferred.	The maximum contribution for 2016 is **$5,500.** If your income exceeds certain limits (see below), your allowable contribution may be reduced or eliminated. (It is possible to convert a Traditional IRA into a Roth IRA even if your income exceeds the limit, but you would need to pay income tax on the money in the year you do the conversion.)
Catch-up contri-bution*	At 50 or older, can contribute an additional **$6,000** to 401(k) in 2016.	If 50 or older, can contribute an additional **$1,000** in 2016.	If you are 50 or older, you can contribute an additional **$1,000** in 2016.
With-drawals (W/D) or dis-tributions	W/Ds or "distributions" **taxed** as ordinary income. before age 59½ W/Ds subject to **tax penalty**.	W/Ds **taxed** as ordinary income. W/Ds before age 59½ are subject to **tax penalty**.	W/Ds of contributions are **untaxed**. W/Ds of earnings are **untaxed** if > than age 59½ & have had the Roth for 5 yrs+. W/Ds of earnings < age 59½ taxed & penalized.

	401(k)	Traditional IRA	Roth IRA
Income limits**	No income limit. Anyone can contribute the maximum as long as they earned that much in wages that year.	**If covered by a retirement plan at work** & income >$61,000 if single or >$184,000 if married, then tax-deferred contribution limited - the higher your income, the less can contribute tax-deferred. If make > $71,000 if single or >$118,000 if married, none of contribution is tax-deferred. **If not covered by retirement plan at work,** then can make the full tax-deferred contribution, regardless of income. **In either case,** can contribute money on top of tax-deferred contribution - even over $5,500 limit - but excess is **not tax-deferred**.	If you're single, your allowable Roth IRA contribution is *reduced* if you make more than $117,000 a year, and you *can't contribute at all* if you make more than $132,000 (2016). If you're married, the corresponding limits are $184,000 and $194,000. These limits apply **regardless** of whether you are covered by a retirement plan at work.
With-drawals	Withdrawals (aka "distributions") **taxed** as ordinary income. Withdrawals before age 59½ subject to additional **tax penalty,** but penalty may be waived in certain cases.	Withdrawals **taxed** as ordinary income. Withdrawals before age 59½ are subject to **tax penalty,** but the penalty can be waived in certain cases.	Withdrawals of contributions are **untaxed.** Withdrawals of investment earnings are **untaxed** if you are older than 59½ & have had the Roth for 5 yrs+. Withdrawals of earnings before 59½ are taxed and penalized.

*The $5,500 annual maximum is a *combined* limit for *all* of an individual's IRAs — both Traditional and Roth. In other words, you can put a *total* of $5,500 in your Traditional and Roth IRAs, not $5,500 in *both* in one year.

**As with the regular contribution limit, the $1,000 cap on catch-up contributions is a *combined* limit that applies to *all* of an individual's IRAs.

In addition to IRAs and 401(k)s, you want to try and save in non-tax-advantaged accounts as well to ensure that you'll have enough money when you retire. Chapters 1 and 2 discuss savings, money market, mutual fund, and brokerage accounts as places to save and grow your money. Ideally, you'll save for retirement in these types of accounts in addition to your accounts that are specifically for retirement.

HOUSING (INCLUDING THE POSSIBLE NEED FOR NURSING HOME CARE)

Where will you live in retirement? If you own your own home and can afford the taxes, insurance, and upkeep, you can live there without needing to come up with monthly rent or mortgage payments. If you're renting or still paying your mortgage, you'll need to figure out how to make those payments each month after you no longer bring home a paycheck. A reverse mortgage, as I talked about in the retirement income section earlier, could be a way to let you stay in your current home while supplementing your other income. As discussed above, you can calculate your monthly Social Security retirement benefit and know how much money you'll be getting from that source. What can you do if you don't have enough money to pay your rent or your mortgage after you retire?

Depending on your total income, existing assets, and the state you live in, you may qualify for various types of government assistance. If you're on the edge financially, it's worth your time and energy to explore those options. Visit the local department of health and social services. Talk to a representative at your area council on aging. If you aren't able to find out who can help you, go to the public library and talk with a reference librarian there. The American Association for Retired Persons (AARP) has great resources online to learn more about public benefits as shown in the notes and in Appendix 3.[129]

If you don't qualify for benefits, you could consider downsizing to a smaller house or rental unit. It may also work for you to move in with or nearer to one of your children or a niece or nephew you are close to. It's not unreasonable to think of getting a roommate. In New York City where our daughter lives, adults of all ages live with other un-related adults with whom they may or may not be friends. It's too expensive for many people to live alone there, so no one thinks it's odd for grown-ups to have roommates. You can too, even if you are 80+, and it's a great way to save money if you need to.

Another housing consideration as you age is the possibility that you will need some form of long-term care because you are unable to take care of yourself. No one wants to think about that eventuality, but experts estimate that 70% of people over 65 will need long-term care support. Buying long-term care insurance is one way to hedge against the costs, which can be devastating if you or a loved one needs years of institutional care for Alzheimer's disease.

Long-term care insurance (LTCi) is discussed in Chapter 1. Unlike auto or health insurance, which everyone needs, LTCi may not be necessary for you. People with substantial assets and people with few assets tend not to need to purchase LTCi. In the case of the wealthy, they'll be able to afford their long-term care. People who are close to the poverty line will likely be driven to a socioeconomic level where they will be eligible for Medicaid, which pays for long-term care. Keep in mind the difference between Medicare, which is the health insurance you use when you turn 65 and Medicaid, which is the government's health care support for people in poverty of all ages. If you have enough money to choose the nursing home you like, then go there; you'll have a greater sense of control and well-being than if you end up getting sent to whatever place has an opening for a Medicaid recipient.

It's worth considering the kind of care you are probably going to get if you need to enter the Medicaid system for custodial care in your old age. Nursing homes aren't required to accept Medicaid patients, and the ones that do may not be the kinds of places you want to spend your last days. Medicaid's financial head is always on the legislative chopping board, and it seems to me unlikely that the Federal or state government will go much beyond making sure that low-income elderly citizens have a roof over their heads and the most minimal basics of food and medical care. It may be inevitable that you need to depend on Medicaid, but it seems unwise to deliberately set yourself up to have to rely on it.

At one time, consumers had the idea that they should give their assets to their children so that they would appear poor enough to qualify for Medicaid and get free long-term care. The "spend your assets down" to qualify for Medicaid trend of the late 1990s and early 2000s seems to have run its course. While the idea of "free care" seems appealing, the reality is more chilling. Any time the government is responsible for your health and welfare, you lose much of your say and many of your choices. If you were to work to spend down your assets and end up qualifying for Medicaid and care in a state-run nursing home, you might find yourself miles away from your loved ones in a substandard room with an unfamiliar roommate.

Even if you do end up needing care for activities of basic daily living, you might not have to go to a nursing home to get it. It may be possible for you to pay for home aide helpers or Certified Nursing Assistants (CNAs) to come to your house and take care of you. If your family is able to lend a hand and supervise your care in conjunction with in-home care professionals, you may be able to stay in your own home instead of going to an institution.

HEALTH INSURANCE (MEDICARE AFTER AGE 65 WITH SUPPLEMENTAL INSURANCE)

Medicare is health insurance for people 65 or older, people under 65 with certain disabilities, and people of any age with permanent kidney failure requiring dialysis or a kidney transplant. It's the insurance that older people use for their medical needs, and part of it is free if you worked and paid into the Social Security system for 10 years. The government website to sign up is MyMedicare.gov. Medicare's sign-up and implementation rules are complicated, but this section touches on the basics.

The four parts of Medicare can be confusing. Medicare Part A, for the hospital, covers inpatient hospital stays, care in a skilled nursing facility, hospice care, and some home health care. Part A doesn't cost people who earned W-2 income for at least 10 years (paying "FICA" tax) because their taxes contributed to the Medicare program. Medicare Part B, for doctor visits, covers physician services, outpatient care, medical supplies, and preventive services. It carries a cost. Medicare Part D, for medicine, covers prescriptions and also requires payment of a premium. Medicare Part C is a type of Medicare health plan you buy from a private company that contracts with Medicare to provide Part A, B, and part D benefits.[130]

You want to be sure that you sign up for Medicare when you turn 65 unless you are still working and are covered under your employer's health insurance plan. If you don't sign up on time, you may have to pay penalties. For signing up late for Part A, the penalty premium is 10% of the current Part A premium. You will continue to pay the penalty premium for twice the number of years you were eligible for Part A but did not enroll. If you sign up late for Medicare Part B, you pay a late penalty premium every month for the rest of your life, along with your Part B premium. The fee is calculated as 1% of the average monthly prescription drug premium (1% of $34.10 in 2016, or 34 cents) times the number of months you were late, rounded to the nearest 10 cents. This penalty is permanent – you would have to pay it for as long as you have Medicare.[131] I find it hard to believe that a mistake you make at age 66 when you realize you are year late in signing up for Medicare Parts B and D would continue to punish you for the rest of your life – which could be like 35 years more if you're long-lived – but that's the current rule. I think that if I were to make that mistake and then be lucky enough to make to 100 years old it would be worth contacting Medicare and asking if maybe 33 years of paying those late penalties might be enough!

If you can't afford your Medicare premiums, your state may help you pay for them. If your monthly income is up to $1,459 for individuals or $1,967 for a couple in 2016 and your savings and assets are below the limit, Medicare Extra Help may cover most or all of your drug plan premium, deductibles and co-pays or co-insurance, in addition to providing valuable extra coverage in the Medicare Part D coverage gap.[132]

LEGACY PLANNING (LEAVING MONEY TO YOUR CHILDREN OR TO CHARITIES)

It's important to many people that they leave some money to their children or to charity. If leaving a financial legacy is important to you, you want to be sure that your will clearly specifies your intentions. Giving verbal direction to others won't guarantee that your wishes are carried out. It's hard to think about the fact that you will die someday, so people often put off actions like creating wills and legacy plans. As covered in Chapter 1, a will is important because it lets you have a say in what happens to your money and assets after you die. Without a will, your state government decides who gets your legacy funds.

When you leave money or property in your will, no Federal taxes are due on that legacy in 2016 unless the amount is greater than $5.45 million for individuals or $10.9 million for couples. Additionally, the beneficiary of your life insurance death benefit does not pay tax on that lump sum benefit. It's worth noting that recipients of gifts or legacies are not responsible for paying tax on the assets they receive; taxes on gifts or legacies are paid by the giver. If the giver has passed away, the estate pays the taxes; if the giver is alive he or she must pay any taxes dues, not the gift recipient.

What if you want to give away money and property when you are still living? Most people have heard the term "gift tax," but few realize what gift taxes are. When you give a relative, friend, or another person a gift, the IRS considers it, technically, to be a taxable event. However, to fall under the requirements for reporting and paying tax, the gift has to be of such a substantial amount to be taxed that few of us ever have to worry about it. You can give away up to $14,000 in 2016 to as many people as you would like without having to pay any tax on your gift or having to file a gift return. If you're married, the amount is $28,000. If you do give a gift of more than $14,000 (or $28,000 if married), you'd then need to file Form 709, Gift Tax with the IRS, but it is still unlikely that you would owe any tax on that gift. An individual can leave up to $5.45 million to heirs and pay no Federal estate or gift tax. A married couple will be able to shield $10.9 million from Federal estate and gift taxes. So, you would only need to pay tax on gifts on the amount over $5.45 million or $10.9 million for couples. And, if you pay tuition or medical expenses directly to the college or medical provider, you never owe gift tax no matter how much you pay.

RETIREMENT CONCERNS UNIQUE TO BLUE COLLAR WORKERS

The Physical Aspects of Blue Collar Work

Retirement from a physically demanding blue collar career may need to come a little earlier than retirement from career at a desk. Even if years of hard work have kept you fit, the demands of climbing, bending, and moving may become too much in your 60's. You'll want to plan well for your later years so that you can retire early, move to desk work in your current trade, or take training for a completely new career. Contrary to popular belief, blue collar workers are often able to find work in retirement. You may want to transition from a very physical career as you near the end of your primary working life and then take the skills from your first career into part-time retirement work.

Dealing with Periods of Unemployment

As discussed above, some blue collar careers come with unemployment when you are between projects. It's hard enough to save when you have a regular steady job. When you are out of work for periods of time, you use savings, encounter moving costs, dip into retirement accounts, suspend contributions to savings and retirement accounts, and stop earning the money that you had come to count on. If your career comes with times when you are unemployed, it will help to plan as well as possible and do your best to keep an emergency fund of six months of expenses.

Frequent Changes of Employers

As a union member or contract worker, you may find yourself with a long list of companies for which you've worked. If you are a long-time member of a union, you will probably have retirement benefits through the union. If your field is not unionized, you may have worked for many different companies and have retirement money in several different 401(k) and IRA plans. When you have time, it's good to collect all those plans in one IRA account by "rolling over" the assets. When you leave a company, you can take your 401(k) to your new job or leave it in your former employer's plan. You can also do a "rollover" of that retirement money into your own personal IRA or a new company's 401(k). I covered the difference between IRA and 401(k) money earlier in this chapter, but the term "rollover" is an important one to be aware of. If you take a "distribution" of your IRA or 401(k) before age 59½, you would likely incur a penalty for withdrawing that money in addition to having to pay the income tax on that sum. If you initiate a "rollover" of your IRA or 401(k), you move the money into another similar qualified retirement plan so that it retains its character as a qualified retirement investment vehicle and no penalty is incurred and income taxes continue to be deferred.

Union Benefits

Blue collar workers in the construction industry or law enforcement may have been members of a union for all or part of their careers. Unions protect workers and make their lives better, as pointed out by Matthew Walters of the Economic Policy Institute: "Recent data from the Bureau of Labor Statistics (BLS) show that, on average, union workers receive larger wage increases than those of nonunion workers and generally earn higher wages and have greater access to most of the common employer-sponsored benefits as well. These trends appear to persist despite declining union membership."[133] Walters provides additional statistics about the financial, health, and retirement benefits union members can expect: "unions raise wages of unionized workers by roughly 20% and raise compensation, including both wages and benefits, by about 28%. Unionized workers receive more generous health benefits than nonunionized workers. They also pay 18% lower health care deductibles and a smaller share of the costs for family coverage. In retirement, unionized workers are 24% more likely to be covered by health insurance paid for by their employer."[134]

If you belonged to a union, be sure to let them know when you retire. Work with your local and national union branches to understand the retirement benefits that are due to you and to complete all required paperwork to ensure you get them.

CHAPTER 6
THE FUTURE OF THE BLUE COLLAR WORKER

The future is bright for many blue collar jobs. Although oil production, assembly line, and manufacturing jobs have been somewhat reduced in 2016, the need for jobs in those fields and many other blue collar positions is strong and growing. Let's take a look at several aspects of blue collar work in the future including the:

- Skill levels of today's blue collar workers
- The value that blue collar work holds
- Earnings potential
- Outlook for women considering a blue collar career
- Union benefits

BLUE COLLAR WORKER SKILLS AND TRAINING

The old-fashioned stereotype of a dumb beefcake swinging a hammer doesn't square with today's blue collar worker, who is highly trained and uses his or her knowledge to accomplish jobs that require intelligence and problem-solving. As Jeff Torlina points out, "blue collar workers use their brains far more than the stereotypes suggest."[135]

Just because the *reality* of blue collar work requires smarts doesn't mean the *perception* keeps up. Few people have been exposed to the value of blue collar work, which makes it hard to convince average Americans that blue collar work is worthwhile. And it is essential that we do because times have changed. In blue collar work today, "the need for precision—particularly in areas involving capital machinery—requires something other than an ability to show up. An operator of a modern CNC (computer numerical control) machine has control of equipment that can cost upwards of $5 million, notes [Karen] Wright [of Ariel Corporation]. A new hire in this position must have knowledge of programming, metallurgy, cutting tool technology, geometry, drafting, and engineering. Increasingly, the factory worker of today is less Joe Six-Pack and more renaissance person."[136] When perception falls behind reality, it's time to get the word out to everyone.

Interestingly, the blue collar workers of today are much more educated and more highly trained than workers of the past. It can be hard to get a blue collar job, and the best paying ones hire competitively. Journalist Sophie Quinton points out that many major companies are seeking blue collar workers but that they "don't hire just anyone. On the shop floor, the company is seeking high-performing students and workers with technical skills."[137]

As a blue collar worker, you will be trained before you start your job, and you will consistently train and learn throughout your career. Unlike the continuing education required for teachers, nurses, business professionals, and many other workers, your training will be paid by the companies you work for. As discussed in the U.S. Chamber of Commerce Foundation's "Enterprising States 2014" report, "those who attain certification in a basic skills field…often outperform those with four-year degrees in fields such as humanities or social science….These jobs are definitely not 'low skilled' unless you define 'low skilled' as simply not requiring a four-year college degree. Being a good carpenter (56% growth) or a good medical secretary (41% growth) takes smarts, hard work, and dedication….It is becoming clear that such skills-oriented training is a better match for many young people. The Center on Education and the Workforce at Georgetown University projects that by 2020, more than 65% of workers will need some kind of postsecondary training, with those needing either a two-year degree or a certificate climbing to 30%. The share requiring a bachelor's degree will rise to 24%, but jobs requiring a graduate degree are expected to remain stagnant over the same period. 'We don't just need people—we need people who can meet our standards,' observes Patrick Gibson, a senior manufacturing executive at Boeing's Heath, Ohio, plant. 'There's a need for a whole change of attitude. It used to be we asked people to check their brains at the door. Now we need people to be not only skilled, but highly engaged.'"[138] Today's blue collar worker will find challenging, interesting, and well-paying work in any of the blue collar fields he or she chooses to enter.

THE NEED FOR AND VALUE OF BLUE COLLAR WORK

Regardless of our perceptions of blue collar work, our dependence on the end products it provides is undeniable. We need people who are able to build roads, unearth oil, transport goods, service machinery, construct buildings, repair and maintain things, and do the many other blue collar tasks essential to our survival. As a non-mechanical person, I view my AC repair person, the SCE&G worker who restores my electrical power, or the folks who rescue me from a stuck elevator as heroes. When you have a real problem, you want a real solution, and highly trained blue collar workers are the people who provide it.

It's unsettling to learn that the blue collar workforce we depend on so desperately is dwindling. The Manufacturing Institute's 2015 report on the skills gap points out that the manufacturing industry will likely need 3.4 million workers while experiencing an expected shortage of 2 million workers in the U.S. over the next decade.[139] Based on these statistics, it makes sense to create programs and initiatives to increase America's blue collar workforce. Although jobs like hotel clerk and payment processor can be replaced by technology, we still need human beings to tie rebar, respond to crime, pave roads, fix machines, drive trucks, and perform many other blue collar tasks. It's important to make people aware of this fact to encourage job growth and pride in a blue collar career.

One way we can let people know how valuable and lucrative blue collar careers can be is by working to overcome negative perceptions. In a poll conducted by the Foundation of Fabricators & Manufacturers Association, 52 percent of all teenagers said they have no interest in a manufacturing career. Of the 52 percent who did not have interest in manufacturing, around two-thirds (61 percent) of the students perceived a manufacturing job as a "dirty, dangerous place that requires little thinking or skill from its workers and offers minimal opportunity for personal growth or career advancement."[140] These young students had not been exposed to the necessity for and the value of blue collar work nor did they realize the scope of the training required to become an expert in these specialized fields. When people realize that blue collar work offers tangible benefits and gratifying work, it's likely that interest in and support for these careers will increase.

Jeff Torlina goes so far as to say that America's future depends on the revival of blue collar work: "blue collar jobs are, far from being important only as history, even more important for the future. It is doubtful that anything short of rebuilding the productive capacity of the economy will turn around the institutional troubles that plague society."[141] I can personally corroborate the significance of blue collar work. In my years in heavy construction, I understood the importance of building useful structures that made life better for people. I still feel immense pride as a part of a construction team that built several 3-million-gallon concrete waste tanks to safely contain low-level radioactive waste, and I know that my co-workers feel the same way. When you drive by or look at a photo of what you helped construct, you really feel as if you've made a difference. It's exciting to contemplate the opportunities available to blue collar workers today.

EARNING POTENTIAL FOR BLUE COLLAR WORKERS

One of the most attractive aspects of blue collar work is the pay. I compared the wages of average white- and blue collar careers in Chapter 1, and the comparison bears repeating. Keep in mind the definition of blue collar here means a skilled worker trained in a specific trade for which no college degree is required, not a sales clerk or waiter. A four-year college education costs, on average in 2016, over $100,000, and many students need to borrow some or most of the money to pay for it. The average white collar worker gets a job with starting salaries in the $25,000 to $45,000 range and in some professions can count on making little more than that yearly for the rest of his or her career. Contrast that with an ironworker who is trained on the job and can earn $70,000+ once he or she attains journeyman status, in addition to having no student loan debt to repay. Economic writer Bill Path points out that "the middle-skill job growth in this country – these new blue collar jobs – are challenging the long-held notion that only white collar jobs lead to prosperity. While the recession hit some skilled-trade industries like manufacturing and construction hard, there has now been a resurgence in these fields with a higher demand for technicians, a position which pays more. But the negative perception remains and many still think of blue-color jobs as 'dead-end' positions. So, young people aren't entering technical and vocational programs to fill the growing need for these middle-skill jobs. Many of them are choosing rather to overlook satisfying and rewarding careers in fields where jobs are plentiful because of an outdated stigma. The perception about blue collar careers won't change until students are better informed about the opportunities, and the truth, about what awaits them in the workforce."[142] When people begin to understand that they can make more money in many blue collar careers than white collar ones, interest in these jobs will grow.

THE OUTLOOK FOR WOMEN IN BLUE COLLAR JOBS

Women are not as highly represented in blue collar jobs as are men. In the past when registered nurses didn't have to get college degrees, nursing fit into the definition of blue collar work and women were well-represented. Today's nurses need to have 4-year college degrees, so that job doesn't fit into the scope of this book. When I worked in construction, we saw few female blue collar workers in any of the trades. In general, women fill relatively few high-paying blue collar jobs; current data show that only about 2.6% of women are in construction,[143] about 13% of women in law enforcement,[144] and just under 6% are truck drivers.[145]

It's likely that the future will hold more opportunities for women in blue collar work, especially as the need for trained, experienced blue collar workers increases. A U.S. Department of Labor summit highlighted the fact that "women in unions earn about 13 percent more than women who aren't in unions. They are nearly 37 percent more likely to have employer-provided health insurance and 53 percent more likely to participate in an employer-sponsored retirement plan. And women in unions are more likely to have access to family and medical leave, paid sick days, and paid vacation. The benefits for women are clear, and that's a big reason so many women hold a union card. Today, 1 out of every 9 women in the United States is represented by a union. Women are also critically important to unions, and that's why the voices of women leaders are so important to the movement: Women are on track to make up half of all union workers by 2023."[146]

The U.S. Department of Labor also points out that "women face challenges that often make it more difficult for them than men to adequately save for retirement. In light of these challenges, women need to pay special attention to making the most of their money.

- Women tend to earn less than men and work fewer years.
- Women stay at jobs for a shorter period of time, work part time more often, and interrupt their careers to raise children. Consequently, they are less likely to qualify for company-sponsored retirement plans or to receive the full benefits of those plans.
- On average, women live 5 years longer than men, and thus need to build a larger retirement nest egg for themselves.
- Some studies indicate women tend to invest more conservatively than men.
- Women tend to lose more income than men following a divorce.
- Women age 65 or older are more than 70 percent more likely than men age 65 or older to live on an income below the poverty level."[147]

Given the fact that women have more trouble financially over the course of a lifetime, it makes sense that a blue collar career can be a great idea for women.

UNION BENEFITS

Americans today have mixed feelings toward unions. Gallup Poll data show that over the past decade, American approval of unions has ranged between 50% and 60%. Most people probably realize that, as explained by Matthew Walters of the Economic Policy Institute, "evidence clearly shows that the labor protections enjoyed by the entire U.S. workforce can be attributed in large part to unions. The workplace laws and regulations, which unions helped to pass, constitute the majority of the labor and industrial relations policies of the United States."[148] It seems less clear, however, if most Americans would agree with Walters that "these laws in and of themselves are insufficient to change employer behavior and/or to regulate labor practices and policies. Research has shown convincingly that unions have played a significant role in enforcing these laws and ensuring that workers are protected and have access to benefits to which they are legally entitled."[149] Although I personally am convinced that unions are still necessary in the U.S. to ensure fair pay and safe work conditions, I realize that union membership and popularity have decreased in the past 30 years.

My personal experience with unions comes from years in labor relations as an employee of a construction company. I had the opportunity to work with wonderful, hard-working, outside-of-the-box thinkers and doers who cared about doing a great job: in this case to build the best concrete tanks possible. I loved my guys – and my few gals – and enjoyed being part of a dynamic and talented team. During those years, we hired lots of tradespeople from our local unions. As much as I value union representation and as positive as our relationships were, I sometimes went around with my union Business Agents (BAs) in trying to make sure that the company I worked for complied with the Project Labor Agreement without giving up costly or unnecessary concessions. I remember fighting with Bubba, my ironworker BA, over a particular grievance whose resolution hung on the interpretation of one word in the agreement. I jabbed my finger at the word "may" on the paper, hollering "It says *'may'* not *'must'*! Those words do not mean the same thing. I'm an English teacher!" Impassive and unyielding Bubba just looked at me and said, "Well, they're supposed to." I don't recall the resolution of that grievance or the few others that came and went over the years. What I do remember is the union representation's devotion to ensuring fairness in the workplace for the men and women who worked under their agreements.

What percent of Americans belong to unions? The union membership rate – the percent of wage and salary workers who were members of unions – was 11.1 percent in 2015 (14.8 million workers), unchanged from 2014. By comparison, in 1983, the first year for which comparable union data are available, the union membership rate was 20.1 percent, and there were 17.7 million union workers.[150] Other interesting points about union representation include these facts:

- Median weekly earnings of nonunion workers ($776) were 79 percent of earnings for workers who were union members ($980).
- Public-sector worker union membership rate (35.2 percent) was five times higher private-sector (6.7 percent).
- Workers in protective service occupations and in education, training, and library occupations had the highest unionization rates (36.3 percent and 35.5 percent).
- Men continued to have a slightly higher union membership rate (11.5 percent) than women (10.6 percent).
- Among states, New York continued to have the highest union membership rate (24.7 percent), while South Carolina had the lowest (2.1 percent).[151]

CONCLUSION

In considering trends in blue collar employment, it seems that the public, bolstered by economic data, may be beginning to realize how lucrative, interesting, and exciting blue collar careers can be. I spoke with Dr. Susan Winsor, long-time president of our local technical college, Aiken Technical College in Aiken, SC. Dr. Winsor corroborates the information presented here, noting that "the cost of education is high today and not knowing what you are going to do with the education you're paying for is even more costly. It's important for people to know where the job opportunities are as they make college and training choices."[152] She too wishes that "the perception of technical jobs was changing faster. American families and students are still willing to take on high amounts of college student debt without realizing that later on in life it will be hard to pay off that debt while making a mortgage payment, a car payment, and meeting other basic expenses. But by then it is too late to change. That's when reality sinks in and the person says 'I wish I had done something else.'"[153]

CHAPTER 7
CONCLUSION

This book is designed to give you an overview of how to be financially safe no matter what career path you've chosen. I also hope that if you work in a blue collar career, you'll feel even more proud of the important job you do. You can confidently guide your children into blue collar careers if they want to go there, or you can support them in a decision to go to college. If you're stuck in a low-paying white collar profession, this book might give you the impetus to train for a higher-paying blue collar career and increase your earning potential. Regardless of your job, the concepts provided here will help you reach the financial goals you've set for yourself. As former US Treasury official Dan Iannicola points out in "Barriers to Financial Advice for Non-Affluent Consumers," "many lack the 'on-ramp' knowledge that often functions as a prerequisite for pursuing and utilizing financial advice. That is, the evidence indicates that a baseline level of financial literacy is necessary in order to seek and utilize financial advice."[154] This book gives you the tools you need to ask the right questions and skillfully evaluate those who you turn to for financial help.

When I was young in the 1980s, we tended to focus on status and dollars – we worried about what other people thought about us, and we wanted to "get ahead," which meant making lots of money and having lots of stuff. We were more "me-oriented," and we wanted to put distance between ourselves and our parents, hometowns, and traditions. Things are different in 2016. The younger generations of the 2000s show an increasing interest in connecting with what they know, and most of them want to do their own thing with little regard for what "other people think" about their choices. They eat local, recycle, live longer with family, create non-traditional relationships, work from home, and embrace a general emotional freedom from "should" that my generation envies. I admire the delightful young people who I teach, mentor, entertain, hire, and parent. They already possess a sense of purpose and groundedness in their 20's that I am only beginning to achieve in my 50's.

This generation's desire to go "back to basics" essentially makes careers in building or repairing tangible items even more appealing. As Jeff Torlina notes, "white collar workers can feel superior to the working class even as they rely upon blue collar workers for their everyday needs. From the comfort of their offices and suburban homes, the professional class is barely reminded that the offices in which they work must be built and maintained by working-class people, as are the roads and bridges on which they commute. Their mail is delivered, the electricity flows to their appliances, their trash is removed, and their lawns are manicured with barely any recognition of the skills and efforts required to make those things happen."[155] That kind of oblivion appeals to fewer people today. In 2016, people want to know where their food, power, water, and other basics of daily living come from. The need to be present in all aspects of life makes it even more likely that blue collar work will gain in respect and appeal in the future.

INDEX

REFERENCES

"Advanced Manufacturing Training." *Greater Lafayette Commerce.*
    N.d. Web. 28 Mar. 2016.
    http://www.greaterlafayettecommerce.com/news/2012/0
    2/16/advancing-manufacturing-we-have-jobs-here-we-
    have-training-here.

Aizcorbe, Ana. M. et al. "Recent Changes in U.S. Family Finances:
    Evidence from the 1998 to2001 Survey of Consumer
    Finances." *U.S. Federal Reserve Board.* Jan 2003. Web. 7 July
    2016.
    http://www.federalreserve.gov/econresdata/scf/files/200
    1_bull0103.pdf.

"An Introduction to 529 Plans." *U.S. Securities Exchange Commission
    Office of Investor Education and Advocacy.* N.d. Web. 19 May
    2016.
    https://investor.gov/sites/default/files/Introduction-to-
    529s.pdf.

"Annual Update of HHS Poverty Guidelines." *Federal Register.* 25
    Jan. 2016. Web. 18 Apr. 2016.
    https://www.federalregister.gov/articles/2016/01/25/201
    6-01450/annual-update-of-the-hhs-poverty-guidelines.

"Annuities." *Investor.gov.* N.d. Web. 28 Mar. 2016.
    https://www.investor.gov/investing-basics/investment-
    products/annuities.

Arnold, Chris. "Economists Say Millennials Should Consider
    Careers In Trades." *NPR.* 2 Feb. 2015. Web. 28 Mar. 2016.
    http://www.npr.org/2015/02/02/383335110/economists
    -say-millennials-should-consider-careers-in-
    trades?utm_campaign=storyshare&utm_source=twitter.co
    m&utm_medium=social.

"Asset Allocation." *Investor.gov.* N.d. Web. 28 Mar. 2016.
    https://www.investor.gov/investing-basics/guiding-
    principles/asset-allocation.

"Average Student Loan Debt Approaches $30,000." *USNews.*
    2013. Web. 15 Feb. 2016.
    http://www.usnews.com/news/articles/2014/11/13/aver
    age-student-loan-debt-hits-30-000.

Barker, Dan. *Leaders, Managers, and Blue Collar Perceptions.* Print. February 23, 2009.

Barrington, Richard. "Tax Prep Costs: How Much Will It Cost To Get Your Taxes Done?" *Get Rich Slowly.* 9 Feb. 2015. Web. http://www.getrichslowly.org/blog/2011/03/16/tax-prep-costs-how-much-will-it-cost-to-get-your-taxes-done/.

Block, Sharon. "The Power of Women's Voices." *U.S. Department of Labor.* 16 June 2016. Web. 28 June 2016. https://blog.dol.gov/2016/06/16/the-power-of-womens-voices/.

"Bonds." *Investor.gov.* N.d. Web. 28 Mar. 2016. https://www.investor.gov/investing-basics/investment-products/bonds.

Bricker, Jesse, et al. "Changes in U.S. Family Finances from 2010 to 2013." *U.S. Federal Reserve Board.* September 2014. Web. 19 July 2016. http://www.federalreserve.gov/pubs/bulletin/2014/pdf/scf14.pdf.

Britt, Frank. "Academic & Professional Advancement: 4 Pros of Career College Opportunities." *Foster.* 16 July 2014. Web. http://fosteredu.pennfoster.edu/academic-professional-advancement-4-pros-of-career-college-opportunities.

Bucks, Brian K. et al. "Recent Changes in U.S. Family Finances: Evidence from the 2001 and 2004 Survey of Consumer Finances." *U.S. Federal Reserve Board.* Feb. 2006. Web. 7 July 2016. http://www.census.gov/censusexplorer/censusexplorer.html.

Bucks, Brian K. et al. "Recent Changes in U.S. Family Finances from 2004: to 2007: Evidence Survey of Consumer Finances." *U.S. Federal Reserve Board.* Feb. 2009. Web. 7 July 2016. http://www.federalreserve.gov/econresdata/scf/files/2007_scf09.pdf.

"Calculate Your Life Expectancy." *Social Security Administration.* N.d. Web. 28 May 2016. https://www.ssa.gov/planners/lifeexpectancy.html.

"Calculating Mutual Fund Fees and Expenses." *U.S. Securities and Exchange Commission.* N.d. Web. 28 Apr. 2016. http://www.sec.gov/investor/tools/mfcc/mfcc-int.htm.

"Car Title Loans." *Federal Trade Commission*. N.d. Web. 5 May 2015. https://www.consumer.ftc.gov/articles/0514-car-title-loans.

Carnes, Nicholas and Meredith L. Sadin. "The 'Mill Worker's Son' Heuristic: How Voters Perceive Politicians from Working-Class Families—and How They Really Behave in Office," *The Journal of Politics*, Vol. 77, No. 1 (January 2015), 285-298.

Carr, Brian. *Blue Collar Wealth: Money Lessons from the Middle Class*. [Kindle Edition]. 2011. Web. 3 Jan. 2016.

"Census Explorer." *U.S. Census Bureau*. N.d. Web. 7 July 2016. http://www.census.gov/censusexplorer/censusexplorer.html.

"Certificates of Deposit." *Investor.gov*. N.d. Web. 28 Mar. 2016. https://www.investor.gov/investing-basics/investment-products/certificates-deposit-cds.

"Chart of Federal Student Grant Programs." *FAFSA.gov*. Web. 15 Apr. 2016. https://studentaid.ed.gov/sa/sites/default/files/federal-grant-programs.pdf.

Coenen, Tracy. "Red Flags Pointed Directly to Madoff." *Fraudfiles*. Feb. 2013. Web. 15 Nov. 2015. http://www.sequenceinc.com/fraudfiles/2012/02/red-flags-pointed-directly-to-madoff/.

"Compound Interest Calculator." *Investor.gov*. N.d. Web. 28 Mar. 2016. http://investor.gov/tools/calculators/compound-interest-calculator.

"Conversations About Personal Finance More Difficult Than Religion and Politics." *Wells Fargo*. 20 Feb. 2014. Web. 28 Mar. 2016. https://www.wellsfargo.com/about/press/2014/20140220_financial-health.

"Considering a Reverse Mortgage?" *Consumer Financial Protection Bureau*. N.d. Web 7 June 2016, http://files.consumerfinance.gov/f/201409_cfpb_guide_reverse_mortgage.pdf.

Consumer and Community Development Research Section of the Federal Reserve Board's Division of Consumer and Community Affairs (DCCA). "Report on the Economic Well-Being of U.S. Households in 2014." *Board of Governors of the Federal Reserve System.* May 2015. Web. 28 June 2016. https://www.federalreserve.gov/econresdata/2014-report-economic-well-being-us-households-201505.pdf.

Crawford, Matthew B. "Learn A Trade." *Phi Delta Kappan.* 6.6 (Mar. 2015): 8-11. *ERIC.* Web. 19 Aug 2015. https://www.questia.com/library/journal/1G1-405925456/learn-a-trade.

"Credit Card Debt Statistics." *NASDAQ.* 23 Sep. 2014. Web. 28 Mar. 2016. http://www.nasdaq.com/article/credit-card-debt-statistics-cm393820.

Dill, Kathryn. "15 High-Paying Blue Collar Jobs." *Forbes.* 3 June 2016. Web. 1 Apr. 2016. http://www.forbes.com/sites/kathryndill/2015/06/03/15-high-paying-blue collar-jobs-2/#1a845bd46e6b.

"Dialogue for Women in Blue-Collar Transportation Careers Final Report." *U.S. Department of Transportation.* 21 Sep. 2011. Web. 7 June 2015. https://www.transportation.gov/sites/dot.dev/files/docs/women-blue-collar-dialogue-fall-2011.pdf.

Dlouhy, Jennifer A. "Oilfield Jobs Decline in July." *Houston Chronicle Fuelfix.* 7 Aug. 2015. Web. 4 Nov. 2015. http://fuelfix.com/blog/2015/08/07/oilfield-jobs-decline-in-july/#34823101=0.

"Eleven High-Demand Jobs You Can Get with Two Years of Less of College." *Technical College System of Georgia.* N.d. Web. 29 May 2016. http://tcsg.edu.

"Enterprising States 2014: Re-creating Equality of Opportunity." *U.S. Chamber of Commerce Foundation. June 2014. Web. 7 July 2016.* http://docplayer.net/17831854-U-s-chamber-of-commerce-foundation-enterprising-states-2014-re-creating-equality-of-opportunity.html.

"Exchange Traded Funds." *Investor.gov.* N.d. Web. 28 Mar. 2016. https://www.investor.gov/investing-basics/investment-products/exchange-traded-funds-etfs.

Federal Deposit Insurance Corporation. "Money Smart for Older Adults." *FDIC.* N.d. Web. 15 Nov. 2015. http://files.consumerfinance.gov/f/201306_cfpb_msoa-participant-guide.pdf.

"Federal Supplemental Educational Opportunity Grant."
FAFSA.gov. N.d. Web. 15 Apr. 2016.
https://studentaid.ed.gov/sa/types/grants-scholarships/fseog.

"Fighting Fraud 101." *SaveAndInvest.org with FINRA, AARP and SEC.* May 2015. Web. 28 Mar. 2016.
https://financialprotection.usa.gov/files/2015/06/fightin g_fraud_2015.pdf.

"Financial Calculators." *Investor.gov.* N.d. Web. 28 Mar. 2016.
https://www.investor.gov/tools/calculators.

"Five Questions to Ask Before You Invest." *Investor.gov.* N.d. Web. 28 Mar. 2016. https://www.investor.gov/investing-basics/guiding-principles/five-questions-ask-before-you-invest.

Fletcher, Michael A. "Pension Plans, Once Inviolable Promises to Employees are Getting Cut." *The Washington Post.* 9 Feb. 2015. Web. 18 Apr. 2016.
https://www.washingtonpost.com/business/economy/pe nsion-plans-once-inviolable-promises-to-employees-are-getting-cut/2015/02/09/6ac95d4a-a24b-11e4-9f89-561284a573f8_story.html.

Foster, Ann C. "Difference in Union and Nonunion Earnings in Blue Collar and Service Occupations." *U.S. Bureau of Labor Statistics.* 25 June 2003. Web. 7 June 2015.
https://www.transportation.gov/sites/dot.dev/files/docs /women-blue-collar-dialogue-fall-2011.pdf.

Fox, Justin. "Farewell to the Blue Collar Elite." *Bloomberg View.* 6 Apr. 2015. Web. 4 Nov. 2015.
http://www.bloombergview.com/articles/2015-04-06/factory-worker-wages-are-nothing-special-these-days.

"Frequently Asked Questions about HUD's Reverse Mortgages." *U.S. Department of Housing and Urban Development.* N.d. Web. 14 May 2016.
http://portal.hud.gov/hudportal/HUD?src=/program_of fices/housing/sfh/hecm/rmtopten.

Gabler, Neal. "The Secret Shame of Middle Class Americans." *The Atlantic.* May 2016. Web. 5 May 2016.
http://www.theatlantic.com/magazine/archive/2016/05/ my-secret-shame/476415/.

Gabriel, Paul E. and Susanne Schmitz. "Gender Differences in Occupational Distributions Among Workers." *U.S. Bureau of Labor Statistics Monthly Review.* June 2007. Web. 8 June 2106.
http://www.bls.gov/opub/mlr/2007/06/art2full.pdf.

Gottschalck, Alfred, et al. "Household Wealth and Debt in the U.S.: 2001 to 2011." *U.S. Census Bureau.* 21 Mar. 2013. Web. 7 July 2016.
http://blogs.census.gov/2013/03/21/household-wealth-and-debt-in-the-u-s-2000-to-2011/.

Grabell, Michael. "The Expendable: How the Temps Who Power Corporate Giants Are Getting Crushed." *Propublica.* 27 June 2013. 16 Oct. 2015.
http://www.propublica.org/article/the-expendables-how-the-temps-who-power-corporate-giants-are-getting-crushe.

Griffin, Mark E. "A Case Study of Blue Collar Worker Retirement Investment Decisions." *Walden University Dissertation.* 2015. Web. 5 Dec. 2015.
http://scholarworks.waldenu.edu/cgi/viewcontent.cgi?article=1318&context=dissertations.

Griffin, Mark and Steven Tippens. "Factors that Influence the Investment Decisions of Blue Collar Workers." *Insights to a Changing World Journal.* 2014, Vol. 2014 Issue 1, p125-134.

Grunwald, Michael. "The Second Age Of Reason." *Time.* 184.9/10 (2014): 36-39. Web. 22 Jan. 2015.
http://time.com/3204295/i-the-second-age-of-reason/.

"Guide to Calculating ROI." *Investopedia.* N.d. Web. 28 Apr. 2016.
http://www.investopedia.com/articles/basics/10/guide-to-calculating-roi.asp.

"Guiding Principles." *Investor.gov.* N.d. Web. 28 Mar. 2016.
https://www.investor.gov/investing-basics/guiding-principles.

Halpin, Stephanie Hoopes. "The ALICE Report." *Rutgers University School of Public Affairs and Administration.* 31 Oct. 2015. Web. 4 Feb. 2016. http://www.uwci.org/files/file/14uw-alice-report-ind-lowres-10-31-14.pdf.

Hargittai, Eszter, W. Russell Neuman, and Olivia Curry. "Taming the Information Tide: Perceptions of Information Overload in the American Home." *Information Society* 28.3 (2012): 161-173. *Academic Search Premier*. Web. 17 Feb. 2015.

"Health Insurance Marketplace Basics." *Healthcare.gov*. N.d. Web. 4 Feb. 2016. https://www.healthcare.gov/quick-guide/.

Hicken, Melanie. "Retired Union Workers Facing 'Unprecedented' Pension Cuts." *CNN*. 15 Nov. 2015. Web. 18 Apr. 2016. http://money.cnn.com/2013/11/15/retirement/pension-cuts/.

"Home Equity Loans and Lines of Credit." *Federal Trade Commission*. N.d. Web. 5 May 2016. https://www.consumer.ftc.gov/articles/0227-home-equity-loans-and-credit-lines.

Hudak, John. "Blue Collar Dreams: Will the Decline of Manufacturing Jobs Damage Social Mobility?" *Brookings Institute*. 21 July 2014. Web. 4 Feb. 2016. http://www.brookings.edu/blogs/social-mobility-memos/posts/2014/07/21-blue collar-dreams-decline-manufacturing-social-mobility-hudak.

Iannicola, Dan and Jonas Parker. "Barriers to Financial Advice for Non-Affluent Consumers." *Society of Actuaries: The Financial Literacy Group*. Sep. 2010. Web. 6 June 2016. file:///C:/Users/Jill/Downloads/research-2010-barriers-consumers%20(1).pdf.

"In It Together: Why Less Inequality Benefits All," *Organization for Economic Cooperation and Development*. May 2015. Web. 14 Apr. 2015. http://www.oecd.org/social/in-it-together-why-lessinequality-benefits-all-9789264235120-en.htm.

"IRS Publication 970." *IRS*. 16 Jan. 2016. Web. 18 May 2016. https://www.irs.gov/pub/irs-pdf/p970.pdf.

Ivanchev, Yavor. "Student Loan Debt: A Deeper Look." *U.S. Bureau of Labor Statistics*. December 2014. Web. 7 June 2016. http://www.bls.gov/opub/mlr/2014/beyond-bls/student-loan-debt-a-deeper-look.htm.

Izzo, Phil. "Graph." *Wall Street Journal* 2014. http://blogs.wsj.com/numbers/congatulations-to-class-of-2014-the-most-indebted-ever-1368/.

Jacobs, Ken, Zohar Perla, Ian Perry, and Dave Graham-Squire. "Producing Poverty: The Public Cost of Low-Wage Production Jobs in Manufacturing." *University of California – Berkeley Labor Center.* May 2016. Web. 10 May 2016. http://laborcenter.berkeley.edu/producing-poverty-the-public-cost-of-low-wage-production-jobs-in-manufacturing/.

Johnson, Angela. "76% of Americans Live Paycheck to Paycheck." *Sanders.Senate.gov.* 24 June 2013. Web. 15 Nov. 2015. http://www.sanders.senate.gov/newsroom/newswatch/2013/06/24/76percent-of-americans-are-living-paycheck-to-paycheck.

Jun, Fukukura, Melissa J. Ferguson, and Kentaro Fujita. "Psychological Distance Can Improve Decision Making Under Information Overload Via Gist Memory." *Journal of Experimental Psychology.* 142.3 (2013): 658-665. Web. 22 Jan. 2015.

Kirkham, Elyssa, "1 in 3 Americans Has Saved $0 for Retirement." *Money.* 14 Mar. 2015. Web. 23 May 2016. http://time.com/money/4258451/retirement-savings-survey/.

Kotlikoff, Laurence, Phillip Moeller, and Paul Solman. *Get What's Yours: The Secrets to Maxing Out Your Social Security.* New York: Simon and Schuster, 2015. Print.

Kulmala, Teddy. "Jay Brooks Gets 15 Years in Prison After Guilty Plea." *Aiken Standard.* 19 Sep. 2014. Web. 15 Nov. 2015. http://www.aikenstandard.com/article/20140919/AIK0101/140919430.

Lamacchia, Joe. *Blue Collar and Proud of It: The All-in-One Resource for Finding Freedom, Financial Success, and Security Outside the Cubicle.* Print. April 1, 2009.

Lange, Jason. "For Blue Collar America Wage Gains Are Slim Even As Employment Surges." *Reuters.* 6 Feb. 2015. Web. 4 Feb. 2016. http://www.reuters.com/article/2015/02/06/us-usa-economy-wages-idUSKBN0L92P220150206.

"Learning Tools – Risk Tolerance Survey." *BYU Marriott School of Management: Personal Finance.* N.d. Web. 6 June 2016. http://personal-finance.byu.edu/content/learning-tools.

"Lifetime Salary Calculator." *CalcXML*. N.d. Web. 4 Feb. 2016. https://www.calcxml.com/do/ins07.

"Loans." *Federal Student Aid – An Office of the U.S. Department of Education*. N.d. Web. 27 May. 2016. https://studentaid.ed.gov/sa/types/loans.

Long, George I. "Differences Between Union and Nonunion Compensation, 2001 – 2011." *Bureau of Labor Statistics*. April 2013. Web. 28 May 2016. http://www.bls.gov/opub/mlr/2013/04/art2full.pdf.

Mclean, Bethany. "Payday Lending – Will Anything Better Replace It?" *The Atlantic*. 5 May 2016. Web. 28 May 2016. http://www.theatlantic.com/magazine/archive/2016/05/payday-lending/476403/.

"Median Weekly Earnings of Full-time Wage and Salary Workers by Union Affiliation, Occupation, and Industry, 2014-2015 Annual Averages." *Bureau of Labor Statistics*. 28 Jan. 2016. Web. 28 May 2016. http://www.bls.gov/news.release/union2.t04.htm.

"Medicare Basics: A Guide for Families and Friends of People with Medicare." *Centers for Medicare & Medicaid Services*. N.d. Web. 25 May 2016. https://www.medicare.gov/Pubs/pdf/11034.pdf.

"Money Market Funds." *Investor.gov*. N.d. Web. 28 Mar. 2016. https://www.investor.gov/investing-basics/investment-products/money-market-funds.

"Monthly Number of Full-time Employees in the United States from April 2015 to April 2016." *Statista*. N.d. Web. 10 May 2016. http://www.statista.com/statistics/192361/unadjusted-monthly-number-of-full-time-employees-in-the-us/.

"Mutual Funds." *Investor.gov*. N.d. Web. 28 Mar. 2016. https://www.investor.gov/investing-basics/investment-products/mutual-funds.

Nicholson, Jessica R. "Temporary Help Workers in the U.S. Labor Market." *U.S. Department of Commerce*. 1 July 2015. Web. 14 Apr. 2016. http://www.esa.doc.gov/sites/default/files/temporary-help-workers-in-the-us-labor-market.pdf.

"No Degree Required; The Job Market." *The Economist* 411. 8889
    (May 31, 2014): 25(US). *Small Business Resource Center*. Gale.
    USC Aiken Library. 19 Aug. 2015. Web. 28 May 2016.
    http://www.economist.com/news/united-
    states/21603060-many-industries-blue collar-wages-are-
    upswing-no-degree-required.

"Non-Traditional Occupations for Women." *U.S. Department of
    Labor*. N.d. Web. 15 July 2016.
    https://www.dol.gov/wb/factsheets/nontra2009_txt.htm.

O'Callaghan, Tiffany. "It's All Too Much! – Discussion with Dan
    Levitan." *New Scientist*. 223.2982 (2014): 26-27. Web. 22
    Jan. 2015.

Office of Personnel Management. "The Twenty Largest Blue
    Collar Occupations - 2013." *OPM.gov*. N.d. Web. 28 Mar.
    2016. https://www.opm.gov/policy-data-oversight/data-
    analysis-documentation/federal-employment-
    reports/reports-publications/the-twenty-largest-blue
    collar-occupations/.

Owens, Tom. "Why the Disdain for American Blue Collar
    Workers?" *North America's Building Trades Unions*. 8 July
    2016. Web. 1 Apr. 2016.
    http://www.bctd.org/Newsroom/Blogs/Presidents-
    Message/July-2015-(1)/Why-The-Disdain-for-American-
    Blue collar-Workers.aspx.

Paladin Investment Advisors. "Types of Advisors to Avoid."
    Paladin. N.d. Web. 15 Nov. 2015.
    http://www.prweb.com/releases/2004/04/prweb122280.
    htm.

Path, Bill R. "Desk Job Blues: Rethinking Middle-Skill Jobs."
    Huffington Post. 15 Dec 2014. Web. 28 May 2016.
    http://www.huffingtonpost.com/dr-bill-r-path/desk-job-
    blues-rethinking_b_6324738.html.

Path, Bill R. "Let's Be Thankful for Skilled Workers." *Huffington
    Post*. 2 Dec. 2013. Web. 28 May 2016.
    http://www.huffingtonpost.com/dr-bill-r-path/skilled-
    workers-lets-be-thankful_b_4340949.html.

"Payday Loans." *Federal Trade Commission*. N.d. Web. 5 May 2016.
    https://www.consumer.ftc.gov/articles/0097-payday-
    loans.

"Ponzi Schemes." *U.S. Securities and Exchange Commission.* 9 Oct. 2013. Web. 2 July 2016. https://www.sec.gov/answers/ponzi.htm.

"Property Insurance." *USA.gov.* N.d. Web. 25 June 2016. https://www.usa.gov/property-insurance.

"Protecting Your Assets." *Consumer Reports.* May 2011. Web. 15 Nov. 2015. http://www.consumerreports.org/cro/money/personal-investing/protecting-assets/overview/index.htm.

Quinn, Jane Bryant. "Can You Trust a Financial Advisor?" *AARP.* August 2013. Web. 15 Nov. 2015. http://www.aarp.org/money/investing/info-08-2013/can-you-trust-a-financial-adviser.2.html.

Quinton, Sophie. "This Is the Way Blue Collar America Ends." *The Atlantic.* 5 June 2013. Web. 3 Dec. 2015. http://www.theatlantic.com/business/archive/2013/06/this-is-the-way-blue collar-america-ends/276554/.

"Real Estate Investment Trusts ("REITs")." *Investor.gov.* N.d. Web. 28 Mar. 2016. https://www.investor.gov/investing-basics/investment-products/real-estate-investment-trusts-reits.

"Reverse Mortgages." *U.S. Federal Trade Commission.* N.d. Web. 14 May 2016. Web. 28 May 2016. https://www.consumer.ftc.gov/articles/0192-reverse-mortgages.

"Risk Tolerance." *Investor.gov.* N.d. Web. 28 Mar. 2016. https://www.investor.gov/investing-basics/guiding-principles/assessing-your-risk-tolerance.

Rose, Mike. "The Mind at Work – Interview." *UCLA Website.* 11 June 2014. Web. 3 Dec. 2015. http://newsroom.ucla.edu/stories/q-a-mike-rose-on-blue collar-smarts.

"Saved: Five Steps for Making Financial Decisions." *Consumer Financial Protection Bureau.* N.d. Web. 15 Jan 2016. https://dearabby.sites.usa.gov/files/2015/05/saved_fiveSteps.pdf.

"Savings Bonds." *Investor.gov.* N.d. Web. 28 Mar. 2016. https://www.investor.gov/investing-basics/investment-products/savings-bonds.

"Savings Fitness: A Guide to Your Money and Your Financial
   Future." *U.S. Department of Labor.* N.d. Web. 28 Apr. 2016.
   http://www.dol.gov/ebsa/publications/savingsfitness.htm
   l.

Schwartz, Matthew and Barbara A. Ward. "Madoff Verified
   Complaint – Exhibit D." *United States Attorney for the
   Southern District of New York.* 6 Jan. 2014. Web. 7 July 2016.
   http://jpmadoff.com/wp-
   content/uploads/2014/09/2014-01-
   06%20DFA%20Exhibit%20D%20-
   %20USA%20v.%20$1,700,000,000%20Verified%20Comp
   laint.pdf.

"Social Security & Medicare Questions." *The Senior Citizens League.*
   Jan. 2015. Web. 25 May 2016.
   http://seniorsleague.org/2015/social-security-medicare-
   questions-january-2015/.

"Social Security Basic Facts." *Social Security Administration.* 13 Oct.
   2015. Web. 18 Apr. 2016.
   https://www.ssa.gov/news/press/basicfact.html.

Stephens, Paul. "Reading at It: Gertrude Stein, Information
   Overload, and the Makings of Americanitis." *Twentieth
   Century Literature* 59.1 (2013): 126-156. *Academic Search
   Premier.* Web. 17 Feb. 2015.

"Stocks." *Investor.gov.* N.d. Web. 28 Mar. 2016.
   https://www.investor.gov/investing-basics/investment-
   products/stocks.

Taylor, Chris. "The Last Taboo: Why Nobody Talks About
   Money." *Reuters.* 27 Mar 2014. Web. 28 Mar. 2016.
   http://www.reuters.com/article/2014/03/27/us-money-
   conversation-idUSBREA2Q1UN20140327.

"Tax Benefits for Education." *Internal Revenue Service.* N.d. Web. 2
   June 2016. https://www.irs.gov/uac/tax-benefits-for-
   education-information-center.

"The EFC Formula, 2016-2017." *U.S. Department of Education.* N.d.
   Web. 28 May 2016.
   https://studentaid.ed.gov/sa/sites/default/files/2016-17-
   efc-formula.pdf.

"The FAFSA." *FAFSA.gov.* n.d. Web. 15 Apr. 2016. fafsa.ed.gov.

"Tips and Tools." *Insure University through the National Association of Insurance Commissioners.* N.d. Web. 3 Dec. 2016. http://www.insureuonline.org/.

Torlina, Jeff. *Working Class: Challenging Myths about Blue Collar Labor.* Boulder: Lynne Rienner, 2011. Print.

"Topic 306 – Penalty for Underpayment of Estimated Tax." *IRS.* N.d. Web. 28 June 2016. https://www.irs.gov/taxtopics/tc306.html.

Tuchman, Mitch. "Pension Plans Beat 401(k) Savers Silly – Here's Why." *Forbes.* 15 Nov. 2015. Web. 18 Apr. 2016. http://www.forbes.com/sites/mitchelltuchman/2013/06/04/pension-plans-beat-401k-savers-silly-heres-why/#62d6c3191d3c.

"Types of Business Insurance." *Small Business Association.* N.d. Web. 15 Apr. 2016. Web. 3 Dec. 2015. https://www.sba.gov/managing-business/running-business/insurance/types-business-insurance.

"Understanding the Medicare Late Enrollment Penalty." *Medicare Matters: National Council on Aging.* N.d. Web. 25 May 2016. https://www.mymedicarematters.org/enrollment/penalties-and-risks/?SID=5746092aa3638.

"Unemployment Insurance." *U.S. Department of Labor.* N.d. Web. 14 Apr. 2016. Web. 3 Dec. 2015. https://www.dol.gov/general/topic/unemployment-insurance.

"Union Members Summary." *U.S. Bureau of Labor Statistics.* N.d. Web. 18 Apr. 2016. http://www.bls.gov/news.release/union2.nr0.htm.

"Wage and Hour Division." *U.S. Department of Labor.* July 2008. Web. 7 June 2015. https://www.transportation.gov/sites/dot.dev/files/docs/women-blue-collar-dialogue-fall-2011.pdf.

Walters, Matthew and Lawrence Mishel. "How Unions Help All Workers." *Economic Policy Institute.* 26 Aug. 2003. Web. 28 May 2016. http://www.epi.org/publication/briefingpapers_bp143/.

Waymire, Jack. "Trust, But Verify." *Worth.* 12 Aug. 2015. Web. 15 Nov. 2015. http://www.worth.com/articles/trust-but-verify/.

"When I Fill Out the FAFSA Am I A Dependent or Independent?" *FAFSA.* N.d. Web. 28 May 2016. https://studentaid.ed.gov/sa/sites/default/files/fafsa-dependency.pdf.

"Who We Are." *FAFSA.gov.* N.d. Web. 15 Apr. 2016. https://studentaid.ed.gov/sa/about.

Winsor, Susan. Phone Interview between Dr. Susan Winsor of Aiken Technical College and Kathryn Hauer. 15 June 2016.

"Women in Law Enforcement." *U.S. Department of Justice.* July 2013. Web. 2 June 2015. http://cops.usdoj.gov/html/dispatch/07-2013/women_in_law_enforcement.asp.

"Workers by Occupational Category." *The Henry J. Kaiser Family Foundation.* 2013. Web. 2 Feb 2016. http://kff.org/other/state-indicator/blue-and-white collar-workers/.

"Worker's Compensation." *U.S. Department of Labor.* N.d. Web. 14 Apr. 2016. https://www.dol.gov/general/topic/workcomp.

"Worker's Compensation in South Carolina." *South Carolina Worker's Compensation Commission.* N.d. Web. 14 Apr. 2016. http://www.wcc.sc.gov/welcomeandoverview/Pages/default.aspx.

Yoder, Steven. "The Endangered Blue Collar Worker." *Comstock's.* 11 Jan. 2016. Web. 1 Apr. 2016. http://www.comstocksmag.com/article/endangered-blue collar-worker.

"You Have the Right to Make Health Care Decisions That Affect You." *Lieutenant Governor's Office on Aging.* N.d. Web. 13 June 2016. http://aging.sc.gov/legal/Pages/AdvanceDirectives.aspx.

"Your Guide to Public Benefits." *AARP.* Sep. 2013. Web. 15 May 2016. http://www.aarp.org/aarp-foundation/our-work/income/info-2012/public-benefits-guide-senior-assistance1.html.

APPENDIX 1
LINKS TO BALANCE SHEETS, BUDGETS, CASH FLOW AND OTHER WORKSHEETS

Budgeting and Cash Flow Templates

- Federal Trade Commission – https://www.consumer.ftc.gov/articles/pdf-1020-make-budget-worksheet.pdf
- Navy Federal Credit Union – https://www.navyfederal.org/pdf/publications/personal-finance/NFCU_1237.pdf
- America Saves – http://www.americasaves.org/for-savers/make-a-plan-how-to-save-money/creating-a-budget
- Bank of America – https://www.bankofamerica.com/content/documents/deposits/service/pdf/docrepo/Household_Budget_Worksheet_Downloadable-6.xls

Net Worth and Balance Sheet Templates

- https://njaes.rutgers.edu/money/templates/Net-Worth-Template.xls
- http://www.moneyunder30.com/net-worth-spreadsheet
- http://www.cfra.org/files/reap-Personal-Balance-Sheet.xls
- http://treasury.tn.gov/smob/Documents/PersonalFinancialstatement.xls
- http://www.moneyunder30.com/net-worth-spreadsheet

APPENDIX 2
RISK TOLERANCE SURVEYS

The following websites provide free risk tolerance surveys and questionnaires you can complete to get an idea of where you stand with regard to financial risk.

- Rutgers University Investment Risk Tolerance Quiz – http://njaes.rutgers.edu/money/riskquiz/
- **Calcxml Site – What Is My Risk Tolerance?** – https://www.calcxml.com/do/inv08
- **Yahoo Finance** – http://finance.yahoo.com/calculator/career-education/inv08/
- **Vanguard Investor Questionnaire** – https://personal.vanguard.com/us/FundsInvQuestionnaire

APPENDIX 3
LIST OF SAFE FINANCIAL WEBSITES

Great General Sites on Money and Investing
http://investor.gov/
http://www.pbs.org/your-life-your-money/tools_resources.php
http://www.saveandinvest.org/
http://www.smartaboutmoney.org/

Social Security Info – Retirement and Disability
http://www.socialsecurity.gov/
http://www.socialsecurity.gov/retire/
http://www.socialsecurity.gov/disabilityssi/

Home Mortgage
https://www.consumer.ftc.gov/articles/0189-shopping-mortgage
https://www.federalreserveconsumerhelp.gov/learnmore/home-mortgages.cfm

Investing in the Stock Market
http://investor.gov/introduction-markets
http://www.usa.gov/topics/money/investing/tips.shtml

Stock Options
http://www.optionseducation.org/en.html

Financial Calculators and Tools
http://investor.gov/tools

Investing in Bonds
http://www.finra.org/investors/bonds

IRAs for Everyone
http://www.irs.gov/Retirement-Plans/Individual-Retirement-Arrangements-%28IRAs%29-1

Roth IRAs for Lower Earners
https://myra.treasury.gov/about/

401(k)s at Your Company
http://www.dol.gov/ebsa/consumer_info_pension.html

Insurance Info
http://www.insureuonline.org/

Retirement Planning for Millennials
http://www.fool.com/investing/general/2014/10/18/financial-advice-for-millennials.aspx
CFP Board's "The Estate Planning Starter Kit for Newlyweds." http://www.letsmakeaplan.org/blog/view/lets-make-a-plan-blogs/the-estate-planning-starter-kit-for-newlyweds.

Definitions of Financial Terms
http://www.investopedia.com/

Financial Literacy for Kids
https://www.fdic.gov/consumers/consumer/moneysmart/young.html
http://www.mymoney.gov/Pages/for-youth.aspx

Retiree's Financial Issues
http://www.aarp.org/money/
CFP Board's "Financial Self-Defense for Seniors."
http://www.cfp.net/docs/publications/financial_self_defense_guide_for_seniors.pdf?sfvrsn=16.

529 Plans to Save for College
http://www.sec.gov/investor/pubs/intro529.htm
http://apps.finra.org/investor_Information/Smart/529/Calc/529_Analyzer.asp (fee calculator)

Saving
http://www.americasaves.org/
http://www.mymoney.gov/Pages/default.aspx

Avoiding Identity Theft
http://www.consumer.ftc.gov/articles/0272-how-keep-your-personal-information-secure

Federal College Student Financial Aid
https://studentaid.ed.gov/types/scams

Estate Planning
http://www.aarp.org/money/estate-planning/

Women's Financial Issues
http://wiseupwomen.tamu.edu/
http://www.wowonline.org/
http://www.vermonttreasurer.gov/financial-literacy/
http://women.vermont.gov/node/630

Taxes
http://www.irs.gov
Volunteer Income Tax Assistance (VITA) or (Tax Counseling for the Elderly) – https://www.irs.gov/individuals/free-tax-return-preparation-for-you-by-volunteers
Tax Advocacy Pane. -
https://www.irs.gov/advocate/taxpayer-advocacy-panel

Sites on Generating Cash

http://www.kiplinger.com/slideshow/saving/T065-S001-11-more-ways-to-get-extra-cash/index.html
http://www.getrichslowly.org/blog/2007/05/10/more-money-5-ways-to-earn-extra-cash-in-your-spare-time/

Long Term Care Insurance

http://longtermcare.gov/costs-how-to-pay/what-is-long-term-care-insurance/
http://www.doi.sc.gov/609/Long-Term-Care-Insurance

- Bankers Life and Casualty Company
  1-800-773-4760; http://www.conseco.com
- John Hancock
  1-800-377-7311; http://www.johnhancockltc.com
- Mutual of Omaha Insurance Company
  1-803-750-6889; http://www.mutualofomaha.com
- New York Life Insurance Company
  1-800-710-7945; http://www.newyorklife.com
- Northwestern Long Term Care Ins. Company
  1-800-890-6704; http://northwesternmutual.com

Financial Planning Links

CFP Board's "Consumer Guide to Financial Self Defense."
http://www.cfp.net/docs/publications/cfpboard_consumer_guide_to_financial_self-defense.pdf?sfvrsn=5.

FINRA Investment Analyzer Tool

http://apps.finra.org/fundanalyzer/1/fa.aspx

Living Wills

http://aging.sc.gov/legal/Pages/LivingWillAndPowerOfAttorney.aspx

AARP Site to Check on Government and Charitable Assistance

http://www.aarp.org/aarp-foundation/our-work/income/info-2012/public-benefits-guide-senior-assistance1.html and
https://www.benefitscheckup.org/cf/index.cfm?partner_id=22.

List of Websites to Find Stocks That Pay Dividends

http://www.nasdaq.com/dividend-stocks/
http://www.dividend.com/

Websites to Help with Reducing Debt

http://www.americasaves.org/
https://www.nerdwallet.com/
http://centsai.com/
https://wallethub.com/
https://www.credit.com/debt/5-steps-to-reduce-your-debt-diy-debt-reduction/
https://www.wellsfargo.com/financial-education/basic-finances/manage-money/cashflow-savings/pay-down-debt/
http://www.mymoney.gov/Lists/MyMoneyResources/AllItems.aspx

Risk Tolerance Surveys

Rutgers University Investment Risk Tolerance Quiz –
http://njaes.rutgers.edu/money/riskquiz/
Calcxml Site – What Is My Risk Tolerance? –
https://www.calcxml.com/do/inv08
Yahoo Finance –
http://finance.yahoo.com/calculator/career-education/inv08/
Vanguard Investor Questionnaire –
https://personal.vanguard.com/us/FundsInvQuestionnaire

Insurance
Here is the CIS website https://eapps.naic.org/cis/.

"Tips and Tools." *Insure University through the National Association of Insurance Commissioners.* N.d. http://www.insureuonline.org/.

Life Insurance: Considerations for All Life Situations." *National Association of Insurance Commissioners. NAIC.org.* N.d. Web. 29 Mar. 2016. http://www.insureuonline.org/insureu_type_life.htm.

"Life Insurance: Considerations for All Life Situations." *National Association of Insurance Commissioners. NAIC.org.* N.d. Web. 29 Mar. 2016. http://www.insureuonline.org/insureu_type_life.htm.

"A Consumers Quick Guide to Home Insurance." National Association of Insurance Commissioners. 23 Oct. 2008. Web. 29 Mar. 2016. p. 2-4. http://www.naic.org/documents/consumer_guide_home_b ooklet.pdf.

CFP Board
"Terminology." *CFP Board.* N.d. Web. 28 Apr. 2016.
     http://www.cfp.net/for-cfp-
     professionals/professional-standards-
     enforcement/standards-of-professional-
     conduct/terminology.
CFP's "Consumer Guide to Financial Self Defense." *CFP Board.* 2015.
     (http://www.cfp.net/docs/publications/cfpboard_co
     nsumer_guide_to_financial_self-
     defense.pdf?sfvrsn=5).

Information on Blue Collar Skills Gap

Giffi, Craig A. et al. "The Skills Gap in U.S. Manufacturing 2015 and Beyond." *Deloitte and The Manufacturing Institute.* 2015. Web. 4 Nov. 2015. http://www.themanufacturinginstitute.org/~/media/ 827DBC76533942679A15EF7067A704CD.ashx.

"Enterprising States 2014: Re-creating Equality of Opportunity." *U.S. Chamber of Commerce Foundation. June 2014. Web. 7 July 2016.* http://docplayer.net/17831854-U-s-chamber-of-commerce-foundation-enterprising-states-2014-re-creating-equality-of-opportunity.html.

Great Books on Blue Collar Work

Lamacchia, Joe. *Blue Collar and Proud of It: The All-in-One Resource for Finding Freedom, Financial Success, and Security Outside the Cubicle.* Deefield Beach: HCI. 2009. Print. https://www.amazon.com/Blue-Collar-Proud-All-One/dp/0757307787

Torlina, Jeff. *Working Class: Challenging Myths about Blue Collar Labor.* Boulder: Lynne Rienner, 2011. Print. https://www.amazon.com/Working-Class-Challenging-Myths-Blue-collar/dp/1588267563/ref=sr_1_2?s=books&ie=UTF8&qid=1469205476&sr=1-2&keywords=torlina

Appendix 4
Blue-Collar Jobs and Training Information

List of Technical Colleges in the U.S.
http://cset.sp.utoledo.edu/twoyrcol.html

Representative Site for Connecting Jobs and Workers
http://www.readysc.org/

Blue Collar Hot Spots – Major Cities
http://www.forbes.com/pictures/edgl45fmhl/no-1-houston/

Information on Types of Blue Collar Jobs
https://www.opm.gov/policy-data-oversight/data-analysis-documentation/federal-employment-reports/reports-publications/the-twenty-largest-blue-collar-occupations/
http://www.moneytalksnews.com/degree-here-are-10-the-best-paying-blue-collar-jobs/

Representative Training and Related Blue Collar Jobs
(Aiken Technical College in Aiken, SC; http://www.atc.edu/)

Associate in Applied Science – Health Services
Possible jobs: LPN, Rad Tech, Paramedic, EMT, Patient Care Asst., Pharmacy Tech, Medical Coding
Provide direct patient care in a safe, effective manner across multiple settings and prepares students for licensure examination for registered nurses (NCLEX-RN). The course of study includes both theory presentation and supervised experience at affiliating health care agencies.

Associate in Applied Science: Major in Computer Technology
Possible jobs: Computer networking, Internet Programming, Computer Game Design, Network Systems Management

Study operating systems, computer hardware, programming languages, web page creation, database management and system analysis and design. The Networking emphasis provides students with the knowledge and skills in hardware and software-specific concepts needed to install, maintain and troubleshoot today's complex interconnected business systems. The Programming emphasis provides students with the knowledge and skills in desktop and web programming languages and software applications needed to create, maintain, and troubleshoot software systems and web sites for today's businesses.

Associate in Applied Science: Major in Industrial Maintenance Technology
Possible jobs: Electrical/Maintenance Certificate, welding, HVAC, machinist, Tower/Wireless Installation
Prepare to be an electromechanical technician capable of the installation, repair and calibration of both basic and contemporary types of industrial machinery. The program's goal is to produce a graduate with the workmanship, design and problem solving capabilities to allow him/her to excel as a multi-trade technician.

Associate of Applied Science- Major in Nuclear Quality Systems
Possible jobs: Electrical and I/C Nuclear QC; Mechanical Nuclear QC, QA auditing; radiation protection; radiation control
Develop the skills necessary to perform quality assurance and quality control duties for construction, operation, maintenance, and manufacturing activities. The program offers two emphasis areas; Quality Control, which focuses on practices, techniques, and inspections in the fields of mechanical technology, electrical technology, and instruments and control technology; Quality Assurance which focuses on types of quality systems and standards, programmatic compliance audits, continuous improvement processes,

176

management of QA records and documentation, and problem solving/critical thinking.

Associate in Applied Science: Major in Electronic Engineering Technology
Possible jobs: Computer electronics, Engineering Graphics, CAD/ AutoCAD
Support electrical/electronics engineers and other technical professionals in the design, development, modification and testing of electronic circuits, devices and systems. This major and emphasis also includes instruction in science, mathematics and the electronics necessary to support learning in practical circuit feasibility, prototype development and testing, systems analysis (including design, selection, installation, calibration, and testing), solid-state and microminiature circuits and the application of technical data to specific problems in the electronics field.

Appendix 5
Union Information

The AFL-CIO

The American Federation of Labor and Congress of Industrial Organizations (AFL-CIO) is a national trade union center and the largest federation of unions in the United States. It is made up of fifty-six national and international unions, together representing more than 12 million active and retired workers. Unions are about a simple proposition: By joining together, working women and men gain strength in numbers so they can have a voice at work about what they care about. They negotiate a contract with their employer for things like a fair and safe workplace, better wages, a secure retirement and family-friendly policies such as paid sick leave and scheduling hours. They have a voice in how their jobs get done, creating a more stable, productive workforce that provides better services and products. Always adapting to the challenges of our nation's evolving workforce, unions are meeting the needs of workers in today's flexible and nontraditional work environments. Because no matter what type of job workers are in, by building power in unions, they can speak out for fairness for all working people in their communities and create better standards and a strong middle class across the country.
(from http://www.aflcio.org/About)

What Unions Do

Training programs and apprenticeships are at the heart of unions' efforts to ensure that working men and women have a voice in our country's ever-changing economy. Every year, the labor movement trains more than 450,000 workers. Through union apprenticeship programs, individuals gain life-changing skills to do high-quality work and get solid, middle-class jobs, often in new industries with cutting-edge green technology. We also harness public workforce resources to help working people gain access to training opportunities and overcome the challenges of losing a job. And along with employers who are willing to work together to share the benefits as well as the costs, we spearhead partnerships that lead to improved job satisfaction for workers, high productivity for employers and a top-notch, skilled workforce that ensures the quality and innovation essential for competing in a global economy. (from http://www.aflcio.org/Learn-About-Unions/What-Unions-Do)

AFL-CIO Apprenticeships
http://www.aflcio.org/Learn-About-Unions/Training-and-Apprenticeships

Specific Trades
Painters and Allied Trades Finishing Trades Institute - http://www.finishingtradesinstitute.org/
Ironworkers - http://www.ironworkers.org/training
Heat and Frost Insulators - http://www.insulators.org/
Boilermakers National Joint Apprenticeship Program- http://bnap.com/
Electrical Workers/National Electrical Contractors Association National Joint Apprenticeship Council - http://electricaltrainingalliance.org/
Bricklayers Masonry Institute - http://imiweb.org/
Elevator Constructors National Elevator Industry Educational Program - https://www.neiep.org/bst-Default.aspx
Plasterers and Cement Masons - http://www.metamediatraining.com/ICD/
The Sheet Metal Workers International Training Institute - https://www.sheetmetal-iti.org/
Plumbers and Pipe Fitters - http://www.plumbersandpipefitters.com/

United Union of Roofers and Waterproofers - http://www.unionroofers.com/education/apprenticeship.aspx
Operating Engineers - http://www.iuoe.org/training

Manufacturing Training and Apprenticeship Programs
Machinists (IAM) Apprenticeship - http://www.goiam.org/index.php/headquarters/departments/apprenticeship
Ford-UAW Apprenticeship Program - http://www.uawford.com/
UAW-Chrysler Apprentice Program - http://www.uaw-chrysler.com/training/apprentice.cfm
USW Apprenticeship - http://icdlearning.org/

Appendix 6
College, Tech School, and Training Financial Aid and Scholarships

Federal Financial Aid for College and Tech School
https://fafsa.ed.gov/

Pell Grants for College and Tech School
https://studentaid.ed.gov/sa/types/grants-scholarships/pell

FSEOG
https://studentaid.ed.gov/sa/types/grants-scholarships/fseog

Federal Work-Study
https://studentaid.ed.gov/sa/types/work-study

College and Tech School Loan Information
https://studentaid.ed.gov/sa/types/loans

Scholarship Sites
Note – for a high school student, your best place for scholarship information is the high school guidance counselor.
https://bigfuture.collegeboard.org/scholarship-search
https://www.salliemae.com/plan-for-college/scholarships/
https://www.unigo.com/

Appendix 7
Financial Calculators for Retirement and Steps for Evaluating Financial Professionals

Financial Calculators for Retirement

- 401(k) and IRA Required Minimum Distribution Calculator at https://www.investor.gov/tools/calculators/required-minimum-distribution-calculator
- Compound Interest Calculator at https://www.investor.gov/tools/calculators/compound-interest-calculator
- Mutual Fund Analyzer at https://www.investor.gov/tools/calculators/mutual-fund-analyzer
- 529 College Plan Expense Analyzer at https://www.investor.gov/tools/calculators/529-expense-analyzer
- Ballpark E$timate at https://www.investor.gov/tools/calculators/ballpark-etimate
- Social Security Retirement Estimator at https://www.investor.gov/tools/calculators/social-security-retirement-estimator
- FINRA Investment Analyzer Tool at http://apps.finra.org/fundanalyzer/1/fa.aspx

How can you make sure you choose the right financial professional? It's impossible to be certain you've found someone who is trustworthy and with whom you will enjoy working, but you can take steps to ensure that your advisor is qualified and in good standing with industry regulators.

Finding the right advisor will require some research on your part because smart investors check the background of anyone promoting financial or investment guidance. With online databases from regulators and industry associations, you can search and read about financial professionals' qualifications, certifications and fees, and disciplinary actions against them.

Different types of advisors

First, it's important to understand that there are many different types of financial professionals who call themselves advisors, but they may be paid in different ways, adhere to different standards of care and be overseen by different regulators. For instance, brokers generally work for brokerage firms and are overseen by the Financial Industry Regulatory Authority (FINRA), and investment advisors are generally overseen by the Securities and Exchange Commission (SEC) and work for registered investment advisory (RIA) firms or are sole practitioners. A brokerage firm sells investment products based on a suitability standard. It can recommend products that are suitable given the client's age, risk tolerance and other factors. In contrast, an RIA firm must adhere to the fiduciary standard; it is required to recommend what is in the client's best interest. But to make the matter even more complex, a financial company can also be both a brokerage and an investment advisory firm. Meanwhile, financial planners don't need to have specific training or certifications to call themselves planners, and they are not subject to the registration requirements for brokers and investment advisors. Financial planners don't actually manage your money, while investment advisors or brokers directly invest your dollars in various investment vehicles such as stocks, bonds, Treasury securities and mutual funds.

When considering an advisor, you'll want to visit the official sites provided by the regulatory bodies that oversee these professionals: FINRA's BrokerCheck for brokers and brokerage firms and the SEC's Investment Adviser Public Disclosure (IAPD) database for investment advisors and RIA firms. If your advisor also has a certified financial planner designation, you should search the directory of the CFP Board, the association that grants and sets standards for this designation.

The first thing you are checking for at each of these three sites is whether your financial professional is even listed there. If an advisor who says he or she has a particular title or designation is not listed, that's a red flag. You cannot legally operate as a broker or investment advisor unless you are registered with FINRA or the SEC. (Whether you must register with both depends on your business circumstances, but you must be registered with at least one.) And although financial planners don't have registration or regulation requirements, if they use the CFP designation, they must appear in the CFP Board's directory. If you do not see your advisor in the appropriate directory, call or email the agency to find out whether the missing information is because of an administrative glitch. It's hard to imagine that a professional would blatantly lie about his or her qualifications, but it happens. For example, I wanted to connect with a CFP professional I saw on LinkedIn. When I pulled up her profile, I saw that she hadn't stated where she'd gone to college. CFP professionals must have college degrees. When I checked the CFP Board directory, she wasn't listed. I called the CFP Board to confirm. It turns out she does not hold the CFP designation, but was representing herself as having earned it.

Next, you can move on to the harder stuff. You should dig into the details about the advisor and the firm he or she works for. Here's how to search these databases and what to look for:

BROKERCHECK

Details on a broker's background and qualifications are available for free on FINRA's BrokerCheck website. There you can search a specific broker's name, a firm or a ZIP code to bring up a list of local firms. If you know the broker's name or the firm name, you can search directly by typing it in. If you want to investigate professionals in your area, you can type in your ZIP code and see a list of individuals or firms nearby. Once you find the correct person or firm, click on the name and then look to the right to see an orange box that says "Get Details." The page that comes up shows four icons identifying the type of firm or advisor; any applicable regulatory or disciplinary disclosures; the firm's inception date or the advisor's registration history and registration locations; and the number of exams the advisor has passed. From there, you can scroll down to an orange rectangular box that says "Download Full Report PDF." This report provides more specific detail on the advisor or the firm. On this site, you will see firms listed as "Brokerage Firm" and/or "Investment Advisor Firm" and the firm's capabilities, scope and any customer complaints against the firm. For an individual, you'll be able to see the broker's qualifications, registration and work history, and customer complaints. The disclosures section of the full report will be the most helpful in evaluating brokers and firms. It provides descriptions of actions the broker or firm has taken that have resulted in complaints or criminal charges. It also shows how these complaints or other issues were resolved.

IAPD WEBSITE

The IAPD database provides free information about investment advisor firms registered with the SEC and most state-registered investment advisor firms. As with BrokerCheck, if you know the broker's or company's name, you can search directly by typing it in, or you can search by ZIP code. Click on a firm or an individual's name, then look at the tab choices on the far left. If you are looking up an individual, you'll see "Get Details" and can click for a detailed report on the person. This report also shows the advisor's work history, qualifications and designations, and any disclosure events.

Once you know the company that the advisor works for, choose the "Firm" box, type in the company name, and hit "Get Details." In the tab choices that come up on the far left, you'll see "Registration/Reporting Status," "View Form ADV By Section" and "Part 2 Brochures." Check out the firm's Form ADV. This form is completed by all investment advisory firms and will tell you a lot about the company and its business practices and structure. Item No. 11, for example, is the disclosure section where you can see whether clients have lodged complaints or lawsuits against the firm.

The "Part 2 Brochures" tab is also helpful. Of particular interest is item No. 5, "Fees and Commissions." There you can see how much the firm charges to manage your money and whether there is a minimum investment amount. Many advisors take on only clients who invest more than a certain amount. However, other advisors have low or no minimum investment requirements.

CFP DIRECTORY

Although there are no regulatory requirements for financial planners, the CFP Board certifies, tests and supervises financial planners who hold the CFP designation. Go to the CFP Board website to make sure your CFP professional is listed. You can search for your advisor by name or input your ZIP code to find local professionals. Each person's name and profile will come up, and you'll be able to see whether the planner requires a minimum amount of assets. You can also use this site if you want to report your planner for unethical or fraudulent behavior. Although it may be possible to find an excellent financial planner with no formal education or certifications, the best advice will probably come from trained financial planners such as those who hold the CFP designation. Most financial planners who are committed to offering their clients optimal service will take the time and expense to formally educate themselves and prove their knowledge by passing difficult exams.

How to decide

These tools can seem a bit overwhelming when you first start using them, but once you look at a couple of broker reports or Part 2 Brochures under an investment advisor's Form ADV, you'll start to see similarities and be able to make more informed decisions about who can best serve your needs. It's time-consuming to do all this research, and in the end, you still take a risk in choosing an advisor. But at the very least, you'll be able to spot any major issues and avoid working with an advisor with regulatory red flags. Another easy – and important – way to check on a potential advisor is to Google the financial professional's name. It's unlikely that a person would continue to practice even while under sanctions or indictments, but it's possible. A search may also reveal behaviors or actions technically unrelated to financial service but that could make you uncomfortable with that person, such as domestic violence charges or a DUI. You may also discover that the person is active politically or socially in causes different from those you support and thus might not be a good fit for you. An internet search will also turn up articles, books or advice-column answers written by the person, which can give you an idea of the kind of advice he or she provides.

After you've completed your research, your best bet is probably to pick the professional you like the best and with whom you feel most comfortable. You'll be spending time together and developing a relationship, so after you verify credentials and past practices, you'll be glad you chose the best fit with regard to personality.

Clarification on the Terms Financial Advisor, Broker, and Financial Planner

In the 1980s movie *The Princess Bride*, the bad guy keeps getting fooled by the good guy. Each time, he says, "Inconceivable!" Finally, his sidekick says, "You keep using that word. I do not think it means what you think it means." I often find the term "financial advisor" falls into a similar pattern. In TV shows, articles, blogs, books and offices everywhere, people talk about financial advisors. But what they mean by that job description varies. And because there are so many different professional titles under the financial advisor umbrella, it can be difficult to define the term. Even within the financial world, you'll find the term being used interchangeably with "investment advisor" and "financial planner." You might also see the titles "broker," "asset manager," "financial consultant" or "wealth manager." What do all these titles really mean?

The type of advice they give makes a difference
One way to distinguish among all of these titles is based on what type of advice the person charges for. If people charge money for the investing advice they give, they must hold certain registrations and adhere to the necessary regulations. If they sell investment products for a fee or commission, they will need to register with a separate regulatory body. Financial planners, who are paid for the advice they give on budgeting and financial planning, but not on how to actually invest, do not have to register. Any of these professionals might call themselves or be referred to as financial advisors. You'll need

to dig deeper into their credentials, registrations and regulators to understand which, if any, of the other titles these professionals hold. Here's a closer look at few common titles and their legal definitions.

Investment advisor

Investment advisors advise clients on investment choices. According to the Securities and Exchange Commission, the Investment Advisers Act of 1940 generally defines an investment advisor as: "Any person or firm that: (1) for compensation; (2) is engaged in the business of; (3) providing advice, making recommendations, issuing reports, or furnishing analyses on securities." For example, if you're an elementary school teacher and you tell everyone at your teacher meeting to buy GoPro stock, you're not an investment advisor. However, if you start to charge people money for the advice to buy GoPro or some other stock or investment, then you are acting as an investment advisor who must be registered and regulated.

Investment advisors may also help with money management, create financial plans, give general financial advice, or sell financial products. These professionals go by many different names, including investment counselor or wealth manager. Regardless of their title, everyone who receives payment for giving advice on investing in securities must be registered with the SEC or with their state securities regulator. Larger advisory firms with $110 million or more in assets under management register with the SEC. Smaller advisory firms register under state law with state securities authorities. These firms are called Registered Investment Advisors, and the individuals who work for these firms and give advice are investment advisor representatives (investment advisors in shorthand). They have to pass certain industry exams to legally give investment advice. You can look up an advisor or firm you are considering working with on the SEC advisor search website.

Broker or stockbroker

The people who are in the business of buying and selling stocks, bonds, mutual funds and other securities are called brokers or registered representatives (of their firms, known as broker-dealers or brokerage firms). They make trades on behalf of clients in exchange for a fee, commission or both. Like investment advisors, brokers must pass certain exams and register with the SEC, but they are regulated by the Financial Industry Regulatory Authority (FINRA) or another self-regulatory organization. If they also charge for the investment advice they provide, they will need to be registered as investment advisors. You can look up brokers you are considering working with on FINRA's BrokerCheck site. One major difference between brokers and investment advisors has to do with the standards under which they must operate. Investment advisors are bound to a fiduciary standard, which holds that they must always put the clients' best interests first. Brokers, on the other hand, must adhere to a suitability standard. This means the broker must have a "reasonable basis" for believing that his or her recommendation is suitable for you based on your situation, but the requirement does not explicitly state that a client's interests must be placed first.

Financial planner

Financial planners are different from investment advisors or brokers in that they offer advice on total financial health (cash flow, debt, employee benefits, retirement, insurance, taxes and estate planning) without giving investment advice on what securities to buy. A financial planner can help clients figure out how much of their assets they might want to commit or allocate to an investing strategy, but the planner can't legally offer specific investing advice about what securities they should invest in, unless registered. Even when planners have the Certified Financial Planner designation, issued by the Certified Financial Planner Board of Standards (the certifying and standard-setting organization), they still cannot act as investment advisors or brokers without taking additional tests and being registered as described above. Many financial planners are also investment advisors, but don't assume they can advise you on how to invest unless they are registered. Conversely, your investment advisor, whose primary role is to manage your investment money, may not look at the total scope of your financial life including taxes, estate planning, risk and insurance needs, college planning, and other essential parts of financial planning that are necessary for financial safety.

How to pick the right person to manage your money

There are a lot of factors to consider in choosing the right financial advisor for your needs, but here are four important ones:

1. Cost: Will it bother you to pay fees and commissions for the services the broker or investment advisor provides? If it will upset you when you are making money, it will really irritate you when your investments decline. Compare fees – whether it's an hourly rate, monthly retainer or a percentage of the assets you have with the firm – before you make a decision. If the financial professional won't clearly tell you the costs and fees, don't choose that firm. Reputable firms are upfront about what they charge and what you will pay.

2. Size: Do you tend to shop local and small? Or do you love big box stores? If you want more of a small-shop feel, choose an independent, fee-only financial advisor. If you like and trust bigger outfits, go with one of the household-name firms, such as Wells Fargo, Raymond James, UBS, Merrill Lynch or Morgan Stanley.

3. Personality: Do you like your potential advisor as a person? You'll want to feel comfortable with whomever you choose. If you don't really like the person, interview someone else.

191

4. Credentials: Are designations, degrees and certifications important to you? If so, look for someone who is a Certified Financial Planner, a Chartered Financial Analyst (CFA), and/or has an advanced degree, such as a Master of Business Administration. There are other designations out there, but make sure you look into the requirements involved and the accrediting organization.

Choosing a financial professional isn't easy – especially with so many different terms to sort through. So do your research and take your time. Like the wizard in *The Princess Bride* says, "You rush a miracle man, you get rotten miracles."

ABOUT THE AUTHOR
KATHRYN B. HAUER

I fix things. My specialties are financial planning, financial literacy education, taxes, and investment advice, but over my 30-year career, I've been able to help people fix problems with money, construction projects, meetings, sentence construction, culinary disasters, and academic difficulties. I wish I were like Samantha of the TV show *Bewitched* and could just twitch my nose to repair everyone's problems. Unfortunately, no magic erupts when I wiggle my nose. I help clients using my knowledge, experience, and hard work...although I like to think that our working together has its own magic. My experience as a financial planner, investment advisor, lecturer, teacher, copy-editor, writer, presenter, negotiator, researcher, and office manager in a diverse cross section of business, educational, and government organizations has helped me gain the depth of knowledge needed to advise my clients in all aspects of sound financial planning and investing. I've had the opportunity to write for CNBC, BBC, CSMonitor, NASDAQ, U.S. News & World Report, Yahoo, Investopedia, and other financial media outlets. I wrote this book to help people of all walks of life understand the basics of money management and financial safety. My focus on blue collar workers comes from a 20-year career in construction where I had a chance to work with and get to know many blue collar professionals whose skill and dedication gave them the opportunity to earn great salaries. This book was created to help my friends keep their money safe.

[1] Path, Bill R. "Let's Be Thankful for Skilled Workers." *Huffington Post*. 2 Dec. 2013. http://www.huffingtonpost.com/dr-bill-r-path/skilled-workers-lets-be-thankful_b_4340949.html.

[2] Office of Personnel Management. "The Twenty Largest Blue collar Occupations - 2013." OPM.gov. N.d. https://www.opm.gov/policy-data-oversight/data-analysis-documentation/federal-employment-reports/reports-publications/the-twenty-largest-blue collar-occupations/.

[3] "Maintenance Mechanic Payrate." *Payscale.com*. N.D. Web. 14 Apr. 2016. http://www.payscale.com/research/US/Job=Maintenance_Mechanic/Hourly_Rate

[4] Dill, Kathryn. "15 High-Paying Blue Collar Jobs." *Forbes*. 3 June 2016. Web. 1 Apr. 2016. http://www.forbes.com/sites/kathryndill/2015/06/03/15-high-paying-blue collar-jobs-2/#1a845bd46e6b.

[5] Dill, Kathryn. "15 High-Paying Blue Collar Jobs." *Forbes*. 3 June 2016. Web. 1 Apr. 2016. http://www.forbes.com/sites/kathryndill/2015/06/03/15-high-paying-blue collar-jobs-2/#1a845bd46e6b.

[6] Torlina, Jeff. *Working Class: Challenging Myths about Blue Collar Labor*. Boulder: Lynne Rienner, 2011. Print. 11.

[7] Torlina, Jeff. *Working Class: Challenging Myths about Blue Collar Labor*. Boulder: Lynne Rienner, 2011. Print. 108.

[8] Here is the Wells Fargo website: https://www.wellsfargo.com/about/press/2014/20140220_financial-health.

[9] Consumer and Community Development Research Section of the Federal Reserve Board's Division of Consumer and Community Affairs (DCCA). "Report on the Economic Well-Being of U.S. Households in 2014." *Board of Governors of the Federal Reserve System*. May 2015. Web. 28 June 2016. https://www.federalreserve.gov/econresdata/2014-report-economic-well-being-us-households-201505.pdf. 25.

[10] Consumer and Community Development Research Section of the Federal Reserve Board's Division of Consumer and Community Affairs (DCCA). "Report on the Economic Well-Being of U.S. Households in 2014." *Board of Governors of the Federal Reserve System.* May 2015. Web. 28 June 2016. https://www.federalreserve.gov/econresdata/2014-report-economic-well-being-us-households-201505.pdf. 25.

[11] "Credit Card Debt Statistics. 23 Sep. 2014. *NASDAQ.* http://www.nasdaq.com/article/credit-card-debt-statistics-cm393820.

[12] "Health Insurance Marketplace Basics." *Healthcare.gov.* N.d. https://www.healthcare.gov/quick-guide/.

[13] "Property Insurance." *USA.gov.* N.d. Web. 25 June 2016. https://www.usa.gov/property-insurance.

[14] "Personal Insurance." *USA.gov.* N.d. Web. 25 June 2016. https://www.usa.gov/personal-insurance.

[15] "Personal Insurance." *USA.gov.* N.d. Web. 25 June 2016. https://www.usa.gov/personal-insurance.

[16] Here is the CIS website https://eapps.naic.org/cis/.

[17] "Property Insurance." *USA.gov.* N.d. Web. 25 June 2016. https://www.usa.gov/property-insurance.

[18] "Types of Business Insurance." *Small Business Association.* N.d. Web. 15 Apr. 2016. https://www.sba.gov/managing-business/running-business/insurance/types-business-insurance.

[19] "Worker's Compensation." *U.S. Department of Labor.* N.d. Web. 14 Apr. 2016. https://www.dol.gov/general/topic/workcomp.

[20] "Worker's Compensation in South Carolina." *South Carolina Worker's Compensation Commission.* N.d. Web. 14 Apr. 2016. http://www.wcc.sc.gov/welcomeandoverview/Pages/default.aspx.

[21] "Unemployment Insurance." *U.S. Department of Labor.* N.d. Web. 14 Aprl. 2016. https://www.dol.gov/general/topic/unemployment-insurance.

[22] Here is the A.M. Best website: (http://www3.ambest.com/ratings/entities/searchresults.aspx.

[23] If you want to guard against identity theft, you can set a "credit freeze" with the three major credit bureaus that prevents any new credit from being initiated or granted until the freeze is lifted.

[24] "Topic 306 – Penalty for Underpayment of Estimated Tax." *IRS*. N.d. Web. 28 June 2016.
https://www.irs.gov/taxtopics/tc306.html.

[25] "Wills." *Government of Maryland*. N.d. 28 June 2016.
http://registers.maryland.gov/main/publications/wills.html.

[26] "You Have the Right to Make Health Care Decisions That Affect You." *Lieutenant Governor's Office on Aging*. N.d. Web. 13 June 2016.
http://aging.sc.gov/legal/Pages/AdvanceDirectives.aspx.

[27] "Stocks." *Investor.gov*. N.d. Web. 28 Mar. 2016.
https://www.investor.gov/investing-basics/investment-products/stocks.

[28] "Stocks." *Investor.gov*. N.d. Web. 28 Mar. 2016.
https://www.investor.gov/investing-basics/investment-products/stocks.

[29] "Stocks." *Investor.gov*. N.d. Web. 28 Mar. 2016.
https://www.investor.gov/investing-basics/investment-products/stocks.

[30] "Bonds." *Investor.gov*. N.d. Web. 28 Mar. 2016.
https://www.investor.gov/investing-basics/investment-products/bonds.

[31] "Bonds." *Investor.gov*. N.d. Web. 28 Mar. 2016.
https://www.investor.gov/investing-basics/investment-products/bonds.

[32] "Savings Bonds." *Investor.gov*. N.d. Web. 28 Mar. 2016.
https://www.investor.gov/investing-basics/investment-products/savings-bonds.

[33] "Certificates of Deposit." *Investor.gov*. N.d. Web. 28 Mar. 2016.
https://www.investor.gov/investing-basics/investment-products/certificates-deposit-cds.

[34] "Mutual Funds." *Investor.gov*. N.d. Web. 28 Mar. 2016.
https://www.investor.gov/investing-basics/investment-products/mutual-funds.

[35] "Money Market Funds." *Investor.gov*. N.d. Web. 28 Mar. 2016.

https://www.investor.gov/investing-basics/investment-products/money-market-funds.

36 "Exchange Traded Funds." *Investor.gov.* N.d. Web. 28 Mar. 2016. https://www.investor.gov/investing-basics/investment-products/exchange-traded-funds-etfs.

37 "Exchange Traded Funds." *Investor.gov.* N.d. Web. 28 Mar. 2016. https://www.investor.gov/investing-basics/investment-products/exchange-traded-funds-etfs.

38 "Annuities." *Investor.gov.* N.d. Web. 28 Mar. 2016. https://www.investor.gov/investing-basics/investment-products/annuities.

39 "Annuities." *Investor.gov.* N.d. Web. 28 Mar. 2016. https://www.investor.gov/investing-basics/investment-products/annuities.

40 "National Association of Insurance Commissioners." http://www.naic.org/.

41 "Annuities." *Investor.gov.* N.d. Web. 28 Mar. 2016. https://www.investor.gov/investing-basics/investment-products/annuities.

42 "Real Estate Investment Trusts ("REITs")." *Investor.gov.* N.d. Web. 28 Mar. 2016. https://www.investor.gov/investing-basics/investment-products/real-estate-investment-trusts-reits.

43 "Risk Tolerance." *Investor.gov.* N.d. Web. 28 Mar. 2016. https://www.investor.gov/investing-basics/guiding-principles/assessing-your-risk-tolerance.

44 "Risk Tolerance." *Investor.gov.* N.d. Web. 28 Mar. 2016. https://www.investor.gov/investing-basics/guiding-principles/assessing-your-risk-tolerance.

45 "Stocks." *Investor.gov.* N.d. Web. 28 Mar. 2016. https://www.investor.gov/investing-basics/investment-products/stocks.

46 "Guiding Principles." *Investor.gov.* N.d. Web. 28 Mar. 2016. https://www.investor.gov/investing-basics/guiding-principles.

47 "Asset Allocation." *Investor.gov.* N.d. Web. 28 Mar. 2016. https://www.investor.gov/investing-basics/guiding-principles/asset-allocation.

48 "Asset Allocation." *Investor.gov.* N.d. Web. 28 Mar. 2016.

https://www.investor.gov/investing-basics/guiding-principles/asset-allocation.

[49] "Asset Allocation." *Investor.gov*. N.d. Web. 28 Mar. 2016. https://www.investor.gov/investing-basics/guiding-principles/asset-allocation.

[50] "Calculating Mutual Fund Fees and Expenses." *U.S. Securities and Exchange Commission*. N.d. Web. 28 Apr. 2016. http://www.sec.gov/investor/tools/mfcc/mfcc-int.htm.

[51] "Stocks." *Investor.gov*. N.d. Web. 28 Mar. 2016. https://www.investor.gov/investing-basics/investment-products/stocks.

[52] "Financial Calculators." *Investor.gov*. N.d. Web. 28 Mar. 2016. https://www.investor.gov/tools/calculators.

[53] You can buy Kellogg stock through this website: http://investor.kelloggs.com/shareowner-services#direct-stock-purchase-plan.

[54] This is the link to the ComputerShare website: https://www-us.computershare.com/investor/3x/plans/buyshares.asp?stype=dspp.

[55] Here is the website for the PNC dividend reinvestment program: http://phx.corporate-ir.net/phoenix.zhtml%3Fc%3D107246%26p%3Dirol-stockpurchase.

[56] Gabler, Neal. "The Secret Shame of Middle Class Americans." *The Atlantic*. May 2016. Web. 5 May 2016. http://www.theatlantic.com/magazine/archive/2016/05/my-secret-shame/476415/.

[57] Johnson, Angela. "76% of Americans Live Paycheck to Paycheck." *Sanders.Senate.gov*. 24 June 2013. Web. 15 Nov. 2015. http://www.sanders.senate.gov/newsroom/newswatch/2013/06/24/76percent-of-americans-are-living-paycheck-to-paycheck.

[58] Gabler, Neal. "The Secret Shame of Middle Class Americans." *The Atlantic*. May 2016. Web. 5 May 2016. http://www.theatlantic.com/magazine/archive/2016/05/my-secret-shame/476415/.

[59] "Home Equity Loans and Lines of Credit. *Federal Trade Commission*. N.d. Web. 5 May 2016.

https://www.consumer.ftc.gov/articles/0227-home-equity-loans-and-credit-lines.

60 "Car Title Loans." *Federal Trade Commission*. N.d. Web. 5 May 2015. https://www.consumer.ftc.gov/articles/0514-car-title-loans.

61 "Payday Loans." *Federal Trade Commission*. N.d. Web. 5 May 2016. https://www.consumer.ftc.gov/articles/0097-payday-loans.

62 "Payday Loans." *Federal Trade Commission*. N.d. Web. 5 May 2016. https://www.consumer.ftc.gov/articles/0097-payday-loans.

63 Mclean, Bethany. "Payday Lending – Will Anything Better Replace It?" *The Atlantic*. Web. 5 May 2016. http://www.theatlantic.com/magazine/archive/2016/05/payday-lending/476403/.

64 "Saved: Five Steps for Making Financial Decisions." *Consumer Financial Protection Bureau*. N.d. https://dearabby.sites.usa.gov/files/2015/05/saved_fiveSteps.pdf.

65 "Ponzi Schemes." *U.S. Securities and Exchange Commission*. 9 Oct. 2013. Web. 2 July 2016. https://www.sec.gov/answers/ponzi.htm.

66 Kulmala, Teddy. "Jay Brooks Gets 15 Years in Prison After Guilty Plea." *Aiken Standard*. 19 Sep. 2014. Web. 15 Nov. 2015. http://www.aikenstandard.com/article/20140919/AIK0101/140919430.

67 "Fighting Fraud 101." *SaveAndInvest.org with FINRA, AARP and SEC*. May 2015. https://financialprotection.usa.gov/files/2015/06/fighting_fraud_2015.pdf.

68 Quinn, Jane Bryant. "Can You Trust a Financial Advisor?" *AARP*. August 2013. Web. 15 Nov. 2015. http://www.aarp.org/money/investing/info-08-2013/can-you-trust-a-financial-adviser.2.html.

69 Schwartz, Matthew and Barbara A. Ward. "Madoff Verified Complaint – Exhibit D." *United States Attorney for the Southern District of New York*. 6 Jan. 2014. Web. 7 July 2016. http://jpmadoff.com/wp-

content/uploads/2014/09/2014-01-
06%20DFA%20Exhibit%20D%20-
%20USA%20v.%20$1,700,000,000%20Verified%20Comp
laint.pdf.

[70] Coenen, Tracy. "Red Flags Pointed Directly to Madoff."
Fraudfiles. Feb. 2013. Web. 15 Nov. 2015.
http://www.sequenceinc.com/fraudfiles/2012/02/red-
flags-pointed-directly-to-madoff/.

[71] "Office of Regulations and Interpretations Employee Benefits
Security Administration Attention: Conflicts of Interest
Rule." *FINRA*. 17 July 2015. Web. 5 June 2016.
https://www.dol.gov/ebsa/pdf/1210-AB32-2-00405.pdf.

[72] Paladin Investment Advisors. "Types of Advisors to Avoid."
Paladin. N.d. Web. 15 Nov. 2015.
http://www.prweb.com/releases/2004/04/prweb122280.
htm.

[73] Federal Deposit Insurance Corporation. "Money Smart for
Older Adults." FDIC. N.d. Web. 15 Nov. 2015.
http://files.consumerfinance.gov/f/201306_cfpb_msoa-
participant-guide.pdf.

[74] Waymire, Jack. "Trust, But Verify." *Worth*. 12 Aug. 2015. Web.
15 Nov. 2015. http://www.worth.com/articles/trust-but-
verify/.

[75] "Conversations About Personal Finance More Difficult Than
Religion and Politics." *Well Fargo*. 20 Feb. 2014.
https://www.wellsfargo.com/about/press/2014/2014022
0_financial-health.

[76] Crawford, Matthew B. "Learn A Trade." *Phi Delta Kappan*. 6.6
(2015): 8-11. *ERIC*. Web. 19 Aug 2015. 10.
https://www.questia.com/library/journal/1G1-
405925456/learn-a-trade.

[77] Yoder, Steven. "The Endangered Blue Collar Worker."
Comstock's. 11 Jan. 2016. Web. 1 Apr. 2016.
http://www.comstocksmag.com/article/endangered-blue
collar-worker.

[78] "Advanced Manufacturing Training." *Greater Lafayette Commerce*.
N.d.
http://www.greaterlafayettecommerce.com/news/2012/0
2/16/advancing-manufacturing-we-have-jobs-here-we-

have-training-here.

[79] Bricker, Jesse, et al. "Changes in U.S. Family Finances from 2010 to 2013." *Board of Governors of the Federal Reserve System.* September 2014. Web. 19 Jul. 2016. http://www.federalreserve.gov/pubs/bulletin/2014/pdf/scf14.pdf.

[80] "Enterprising States 2014: Re-creating Equality of Opportunity." *U.S. Chamber of Commerce Foundation. June 2014. Web. 7 July 2016.* http://docplayer.net/17831854-U-s-chamber-of-commerce-foundation-enterprising-states-2014-re-creating-equality-of-opportunity.html. 14.

[81] Britt, Frank. "Academic & Professional Advancement: 4 Pros of Career College Opportunities." *Foster.* 16 July 2014. http://fosteredu.pennfoster.edu/academic-professional-advancement-4-pros-of-career-college-opportunities.

[82] Ivanchev, Yavor. "Student Loan Debt: A Deeper Look." *U.S. Bureau of Labor Statistics.* December 2104. 7 June 2016. http://www.bls.gov/opub/mlr/2014/beyond-bls/student-loan-debt-a-deeper-look.htm.

[83] Torlina, Jeff. *Working Class: Challenging Myths about Blue Collar Labor.* Boulder: Lynne Rienner, 2011. Print. 145-6.

[84] Comment attributed to Ryan Lance, Conoco executive, March 2013.

[85] Schultz, Caroline. "Alaska Economic Trends." *Alaska Department of Labor and Workforce Development.* Jan. 2016. Web. 28 June 2016. http://labor.alaska.gov/trends/jan16.pdf.

[86] Fox, Justin. "Farewell to the Blue Collar Elite." *Bloomberg View.* 6 Apr. 2015. http://www.bloombergview.com/articles/2015-04-06/factory-worker-wages-are-nothing-special-these-days.

[87] Jacobs, Ken, Zohar Perla, Ian Perry, and Dave Graham-Squire. "Producing Poverty: The Public Cost of Low-Wage Production Jobs in Manufacturing." *University of California – Berkeley Labor Center.* May 2016. Web 10 May 2016. http://laborcenter.berkeley.edu/producing-poverty-the-public-cost-of-low-wage-production-jobs-in-manufacturing/.

[88] OSHA Construction Statistics. https://www.osha.gov/oshstats/commonstats.html.

[89] U.S. Bureau of Labor Statistics.
  http://www.bls.gov/iif/oshwc/ostb1630.pdf.
[90] Crawford, Matthew B. "Learn A Trade." *Phi Delta Kappan.* 6.6
  (Mar. 2015): 8-11. *ERIC.* Web. 19 Aug. 2015. 11.
  https://www.questia.com/library/journal/1G1-
  405925456/learn-a-trade.
[91] Owens, Tom. "Why the Disdain for American Blue Collar
  Workers?" *North America's Building Trades Unions.* 8 July
  2016. Web. 1 Apr. 2016.
  http://www.bctd.org/Newsroom/Blogs/Presidents-
  Message/July-2015-(1)/Why-The-Disdain-for-American-
  Blue collar-Workers.aspx.
[92] Lange, Jason. "For Blue Collar America Wage Gains Are Slim
  Even As Employment Surges." *Reuters.* 6 Feb. 2015.
  http://www.reuters.com/article/2015/02/06/us-usa-
  economy-wages-idUSKBN0L92P220150206.
[93] "Blue Collar Job Blues – Are We Losing Our Workers?"
  FinancesOnline. 12 Apr. 2013.
  http://financesonline.com/blue collar-blues-are-we-
  losing-our-blue collar-workers/.
[94] Britt, Frank. "Academic & Professional Advancement: 4 Pros of
  Career College Opportunities." Foster. 16 July 2014.
  http://fosteredu.pennfoster.edu/academic-professional-
  advancement-4-pros-of-career-college-opportunities.
[95] Winsor, Susan. Phone Interview between Dr. Susan Winsor of
  Aiken Technical College and Kathryn Hauer. 15 June
  2016.
[96] Arnold, Chris. "Economists Say Millennials Should Consider
  Careers In Trades." *NPR.* 2 Feb. 2015.
  http://www.npr.org/2015/02/02/383335110/economists
  -say-millennials-should-consider-careers-in-
  trades?utm_campaign=storyshare&utm_source=twitter.co
  m&utm_medium=social.
[97] "IRS Publication 970." *IRS.* 16 Jan. 2016. Web. 18 May 2016.
  https://www.irs.gov/pub/irs-pdf/p970.pdf.
[98] "IRS Publication 970." *IRS.* 16 Jan. 2016. Web. 18 May 2016.
  https://www.irs.gov/pub/irs-pdf/p970.pdf.
[99] "IRS Publication 970." *IRS.* 16 Jan. 2016. Web. 18 May 2016.
  https://www.irs.gov/pub/irs-pdf/p970.pdf.

[100] "An Introduction to 529 Plans." *U.S. Securities Exchange Commission Office of Investor Education and Advocacy.* N.d. Web. 19May 2016. https://investor.gov/sites/default/files/Introduction-to-529s.pdf.

[101] "An Introduction to 529 Plans." *U.S. Securities Exchange Commission Office of Investor Education and Advocacy.* N.d. Web. 19May 2016. https://investor.gov/sites/default/files/Introduction-to-529s.pdf.

[102] "An Introduction to 529 Plans." *U.S. Securities Exchange Commission Office of Investor Education and Advocacy.* N.d. Web. 19May 2016. https://investor.gov/sites/default/files/Introduction-to-529s.pdf.

[103] "The FAFSA." *Federal Student Aid – An Office of the U.S. Department of Education.* N.d. Web. 27 May. 2016. https://fafsa.ed.gov/.

[104] "The FAFSA." *Federal Student Aid – An Office of the U.S. Department of Education.* N.d. Web. 27 May. 2016. https://fafsa.ed.gov/.

[105] "Who We Are." *FAFSA.gov.* n.d. Web. 15 Apr. 2016. https://studentaid.ed.gov/sa/about.

[106] "Chart of Federal Student Grant Programs." *FAFSA.gov.* Web. 15 Apr. 2016. https://studentaid.ed.gov/sa/sites/default/files/federal-grant-programs.pdf.

[107] "The FAFSA." *Federal Student Aid – An Office of the U.S. Department of Education.* N.d. Web. 27 May. 2016. https://fafsa.ed.gov/.

[108] "The EFC Formula, 2016-2017." *U.S. Department of Education.* N.d. Web. 28 May 2016. https://studentaid.ed.gov/sa/sites/default/files/2016-17-efc-formula.pdf.

[109] "The EFC Formula, 2016-2017." *U.S. Department of Education.* N.d. Web. 28 May 2016. https://studentaid.ed.gov/sa/sites/default/files/2016-17-efc-formula.pdf.

[110] "The FAFSA." *FAFSA.gov.* n.d. Web. 15 Apr. 2016.

fafsa.ed.gov.

[111] "Federal Supplemental Educational Opportunity Grant."
FAFSA.gov. n.d. Web. 15 Apr. 2016.
https://studentaid.ed.gov/sa/types/grants-
scholarships/fseog.

[112] "Loans." *Federal Student Aid – An Office of the U.S. Department of
Education.* N.d. Web. 27 May. 2016.
https://studentaid.ed.gov/sa/types/loans.

[113] "Loans." *Federal Student Aid – An Office of the U.S. Department of
Education.* N.d. Web. 27 May. 2016.
https://studentaid.ed.gov/sa/types/loans.

[114] "When I Fill Out the FAFSA Am I A Dependent or
Independent?" N.d. Web. 28 May 2016.
https://studentaid.ed.gov/sa/sites/default/files/fafsa-
dependency.pdf.

[115] "Tax Benefits for Education." *Internal Revenue Service.* N.d. Web.
2 June 2016. https://www.irs.gov/uac/tax-benefits-for-
education-information-center.

[116] "Social Security Basic Facts." *Social Security Administration.* 13
Oct. 2015. Web. 18 Apr. 2016.
https://www.ssa.gov/news/press/basicfact.html.

[117] "Annual Update of HHS Poverty Guidelines." *Federal Register.* 25
Jan. 2016. Web. 18 Apr. 2016.
https://www.federalregister.gov/articles/2016/01/25/201
6-01450/annual-update-of-the-hhs-poverty-guidelines.

[118] Kotlikoff, Laurence, Phillip Moeller, and Paul Solman. *Get
What's Yours: The Secrets to Maxing Out Your Social Security.*
New York: Simon and Schuster, 2015. Print.

[119] "Calculate Your Life Expectancy." *Social Security Administration.*
N.d. Web. 28 May 2016.
https://www.ssa.gov/planners/lifeexpectancy.html.

[120] Here is the AARP website for researching possible government
assistance you might qualify for:
http://www.aarp.org/aarp-foundation/our-
work/income/info-2012/public-benefits-guide-senior-
assistance1.html).

[121] "Considering a Reverse Mortgage?" *Consumer Financial Protection
Bureau.* N.d. Web 7 June 2016,
http://files.consumerfinance.gov/f/201409_cfpb_guide_r

everse_mortgage.pdf.

122 "Frequently Asked Questions about HUD's Reverse Mortgages." *U.S. Department of Housing and Urban Development*. N.d. Web. 14 May 2016. http://portal.hud.gov/hudportal/HUD?src=/program_of fices/housing/sfh/hecm/rmtopten.

123 "Reverse Mortgages." *U.S. Federal Trade Commission*. N.d. Web. 14 May 2016. https://www.consumer.ftc.gov/articles/0192-reverse-mortgages.

124 Here is the IRS website that provides RMD tables: https://www.irs.gov/retirement-plans/plan-participant-employee/retirement-topics-required-minimum-distributions-rmds.

125 Tuchman, Mitch. "Pension Plans Beat 401(k) Savers Silly – Here's Why." *Forbes*. 15 Nov. 2015. Web. 18 Apr. 2016. http://www.forbes.com/sites/mitchelltuchman/2013/06/04/pension-plans-beat-401k-savers-silly-heres-why/#62d6c3191d3c.

126 Fletcher, Michael A. "Pension Plans Getting Cut." *The Washington Post*. 9 Feb. 2015. Web. 18 Apr. 2016. https://www.washingtonpost.com/business/economy/pension-plans-once-inviolable-promises-to-employees-are-getting-cut/2015/02/09/6ac95d4a-a24b-11e4-9f89-561284a573f8_story.html.

127 Kirkham, Elyssa, "1 in 3 Americans Has Saved $0 for Retirement." *Money*. 14 Mar. 2015. Web. 23 May 2016. http://time.com/money/4258451/retirement-savings-survey/.

128 Kirkham, Elyssa, "1 in 3 Americans Has Saved $0 for Retirement." *Money*. 14 Mar. 2015. Web. 23 May 2016. http://time.com/money/4258451/retirement-savings-survey/.

129 "Your Guide to Public Benefits." *AARP*. Sep. 2013. Web. 15 May 2016. http://www.aarp.org/aarp-foundation/our-work/income/info-2012/public-benefits-guide-senior-assistance1.html and https://www.benefitscheckup.org/cf/index.cfm?partner_i d=22.

[130] "Medicare Basics: A Guide for Families and Friends of People with Medicare." Centers for Medicare & Medicaid Services. N.d. Web. 25 May 2016. https://www.medicare.gov/Pubs/pdf/11034.pdf.

[131] "Understanding the Medicare Late Enrollment Penalty." *Medicare Matters: National Council on Aging.* N.d. Web. 25 May 2016. https://www.mymedicarematters.org/enrollment/penalties-and-risks/?SID=5746092aa3638.

[132] "Social Security & Medicare Questions." *The Senior Citizens League.* Jan. 2015. Web. 25 May 2016. http://seniorsleague.org/2015/social-security-medicare-questions-january-2015/.

[133] Long, George I. "Differences Between Union and Nonunion Compensation, 2001 – 2011." *Bureau of Labor Statistics.* April 2013. Web. 28 May 2016. http://www.bls.gov/opub/mlr/2013/04/art2full.pdf.

[134] Walters, Matthew and Lawrence Mishel. "How Unions Help All Workers." *Economic Policy Institute.* 26 Aug. 2003. Web. 28 May 2016. http://www.epi.org/publication/briefingpapers_bp143/.

[135] Torlina, Jeff. *Working Class: Challenging Myths about Blue collar Labor.* Boulder: Lynne Rienner, 2011. Print. 13.

[136] "Enterprising States 2014: Re-creating Equality of Opportunity." *U.S. Chamber of Commerce Foundation.* June 2014. Web. 7 July 2016. http://docplayer.net/17831854-U-s-chamber-of-commerce-foundation-enterprising-states-2014-re-creating-equality-of-opportunity.html. 18.

[137] Quinton, Sophie. "This Is the Way Blue Collar America Ends." *The Altantic.* 5 June 2013. http://www.theatlantic.com/business/archive/2013/06/this-is-the-way-blue collar-america-ends/276554/.

[138] "Enterprising States 2014: Re-creating Equality of Opportunity." *U.S. Chamber of Commerce Foundation.* June 2014. Web. 7 July 2016. http://docplayer.net/17831854-U-s-chamber-of-commerce-foundation-enterprising-states-2014-re-creating-equality-of-opportunity.html. 11.

[139] Giffi, Craig A. et al. "The Skills Gap in U.S. Manufacturing 2015 and Beyond." *Deloitte and The Manufacturing Institute.* 2015.

http://www.themanufacturinginstitute.org/~/media/827
DBC76533942679A15EF7067A704CD.ashx. 25.

[140] Giffi, Craig A. et al. "The Skills Gap in U.S. Manufacturing 2015 and Beyond." *Deloitte and The Manufacturing Institute*. 2015. http://www.themanufacturinginstitute.org/~/media/827 DBC76533942679A15EF7067A704CD.ashx. 15.

[141] Torlina, Jeff. *Working Class: Challenging Myths about Blue collar Labor.* Boulder: Lynne Rienner, 2011. Print. 188.

[142] Path, Bill R. "Desk Job Blues: Rethinking Middle-Skill Jobs." *Huffington Post*. 15 Dec 2014. http://www.huffingtonpost.com/dr-bill-r-path/desk-job-blues-rethinking_b_6324738.html.

[143] Gabriel, Paul E. and Susanne Schmitz. "Gender Differences in Occupational Distributions Among Workers." *U.S. Bureau of Labor Statistics Monthly Review*. June 2007. Web. 8 June 2106. http://www.bls.gov/opub/mlr/2007/06/art2full.pdf.

[144] "Women in Law Enforcement." *U.S. Department of Justice*. July 2013. Web. 2 June 2015. http://cops.usdoj.gov/html/dispatch/07-2013/women_in_law_enforcement.asp.

[145] "Non-Traditional Occupations for Women." *U.S. Department of Labor*. N.d. Web. 15 July 2016. https://www.dol.gov/wb/factsheets/nontra2009_txt.htm.

[146] Block, Sharon. "The Power of Women's Voices." *U.S. Department of Labor*. 16 June 2016. Web. 28 June 2016. https://blog.dol.gov/2016/06/16/the-power-of-womens-voices/.

[147] "Savings Fitness: A Guide to Your Money and Your Financial Future." *U.S. Department of Labor*. N.d. Web 28 Apr. 2016. http://www.dol.gov/ebsa/publications/savingsfitness.html.

[148] Walters, Matthew and Lawrence Mishel. "How Unions Help All Workers." *Economic Policy Institute*. 26 Aug. 2003. Web. 28 May 2016. http://www.epi.org/publication/briefingpapers_bp143/.

[149] Walters, Matthew and Lawrence Mishel. "How Unions Help All Workers." *Economic Policy Institute*. 26 Aug. 2003. Web. 28 May 2016.

http://www.epi.org/publication/briefingpapers_bp143/.

[150] "Union Members Summary." *U.S. Bureau of Labor Statistics.* N.d. Web. 18 Apr. 2016. http://www.bls.gov/news.release/union2.nr0.htm.

[151] "Union Members Summary." *U.S. Bureau of Labor Statistics.* N.d. Web. 18 Apr. 2016. http://www.bls.gov/news.release/union2.nr0.htm.

[152] Winsor, Susan. Phone Interview between Dr. Susan Winsor of Aiken Technical College and Kathryn Hauer. 15 June 2016.

[153] Winsor, Susan. Phone Interview between Dr. Susan Winsor of Aiken Technical College and Kathryn Hauer. 15 June 2016.

[154] Iannicola, Dan and Jonas Parker. "Barriers to Financial Advice for Non-Affluent Consumers." *Society of Actuaries: The Financial Literacy Group.* Sep. 2010. Web. 6 June 2016. file:///C:/Users/Jill/Downloads/research-2010-barriers-consumers%20(1).pdf.

[155] Torlina, Jeff. *Working Class: Challenging Myths about Blue Collar Labor.* Boulder: Lynne Rienner, 2011. Print. 187.